Summer Abstract

Coloring Book

Original Hand Drawn Images for Relaxation

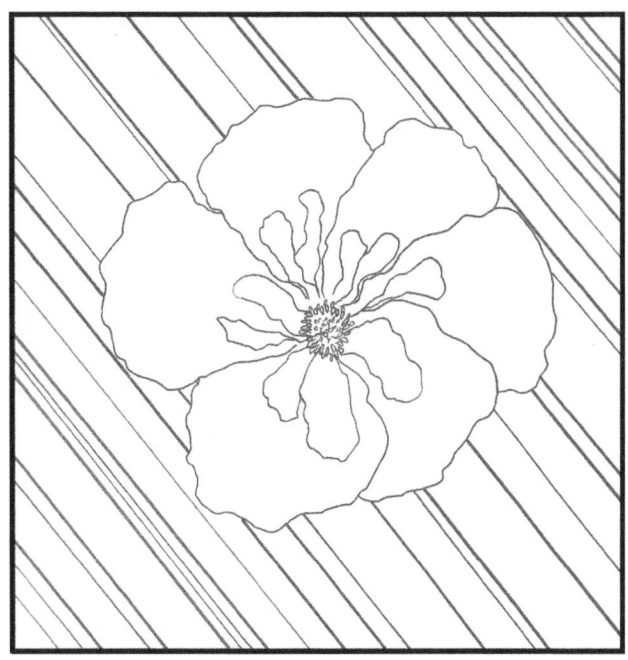

By: Kaye Dennan

KD Coloring Studio

http://kdcoloring.com

ISBN-13: 978-1533265029

Sample Graphics from this Book

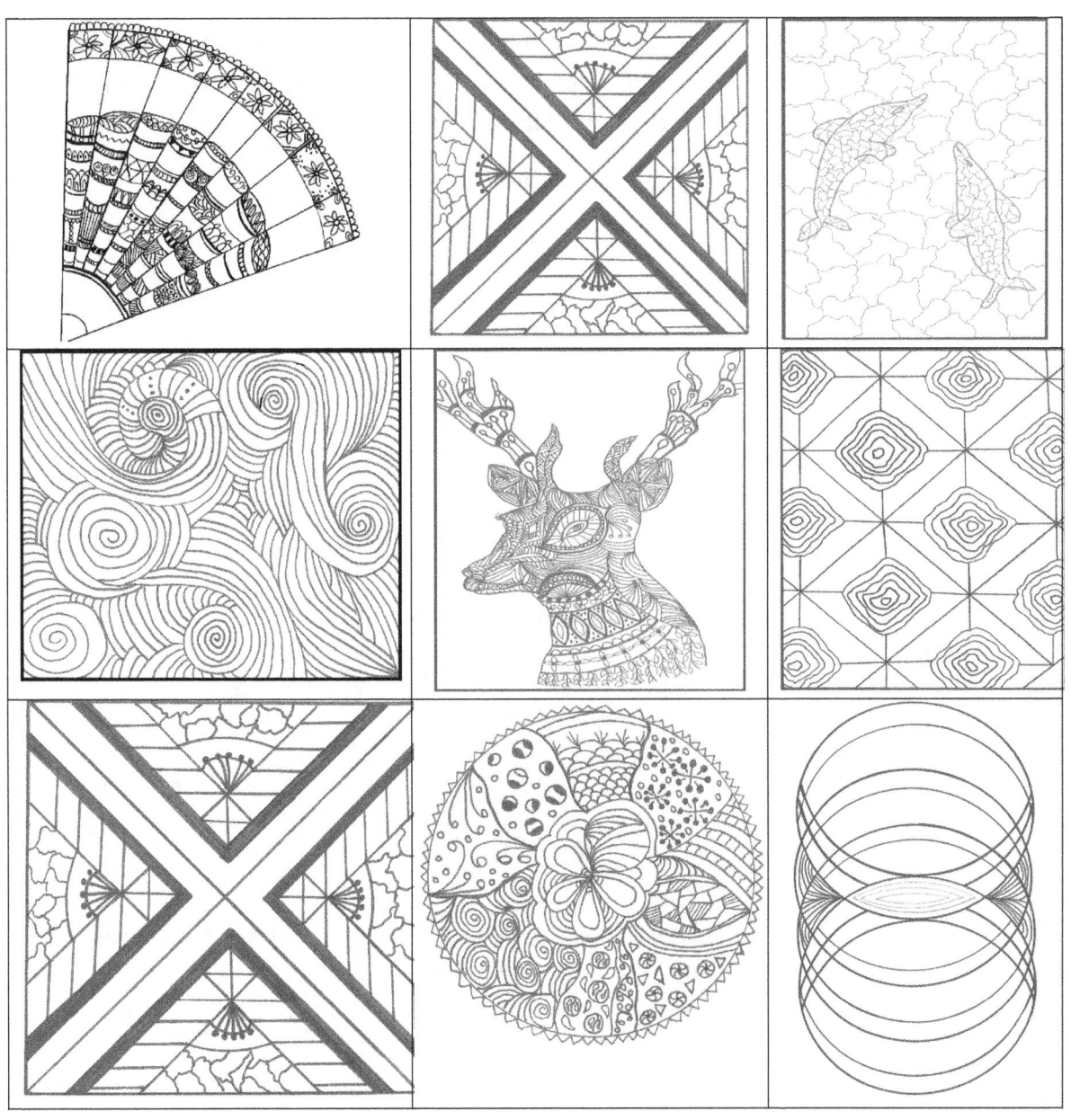

PUBLISHERS NOTES
Disclaimer

Paperback Edition

Manufactured in the United States of America

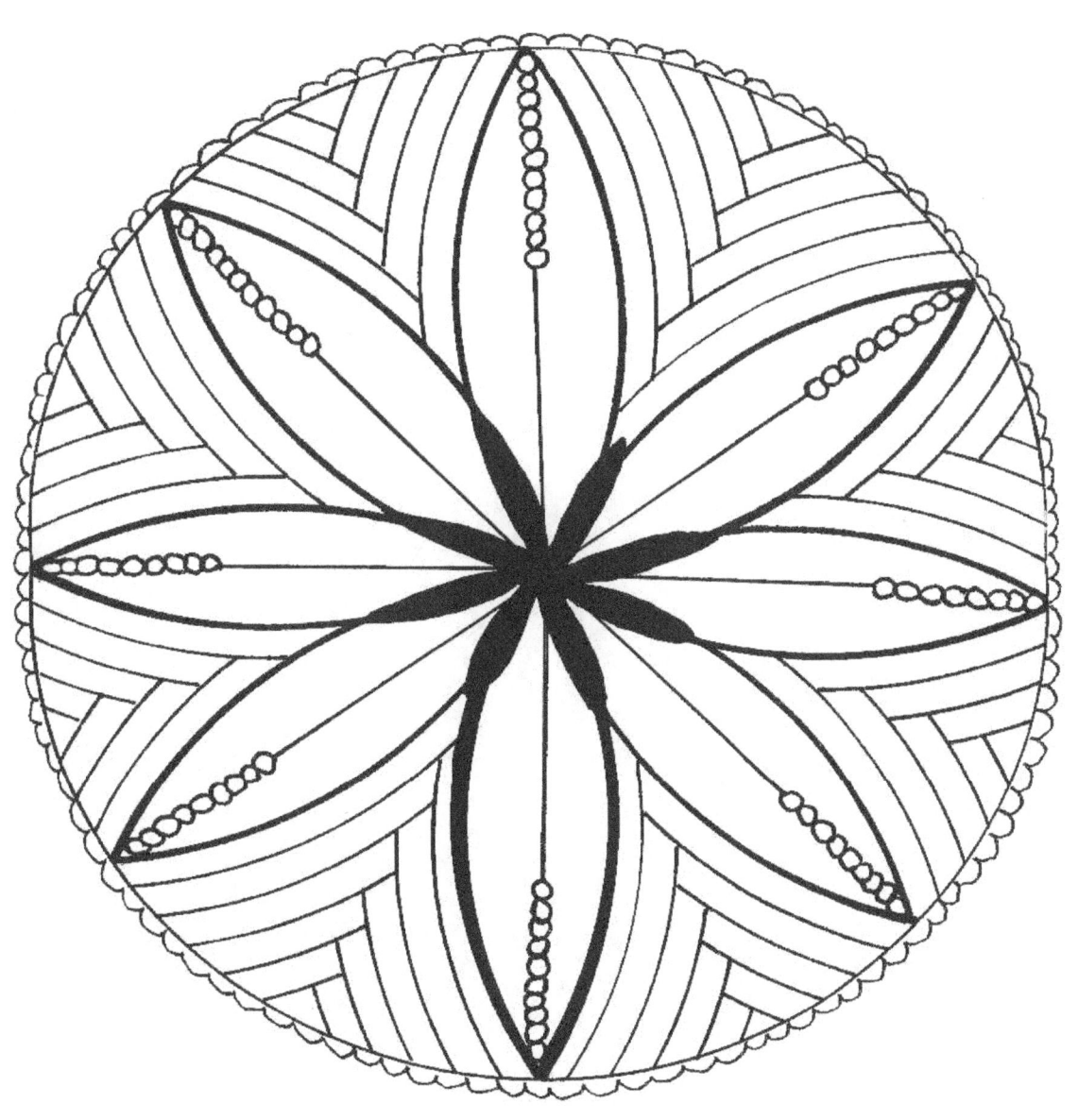

Kaye Dennan

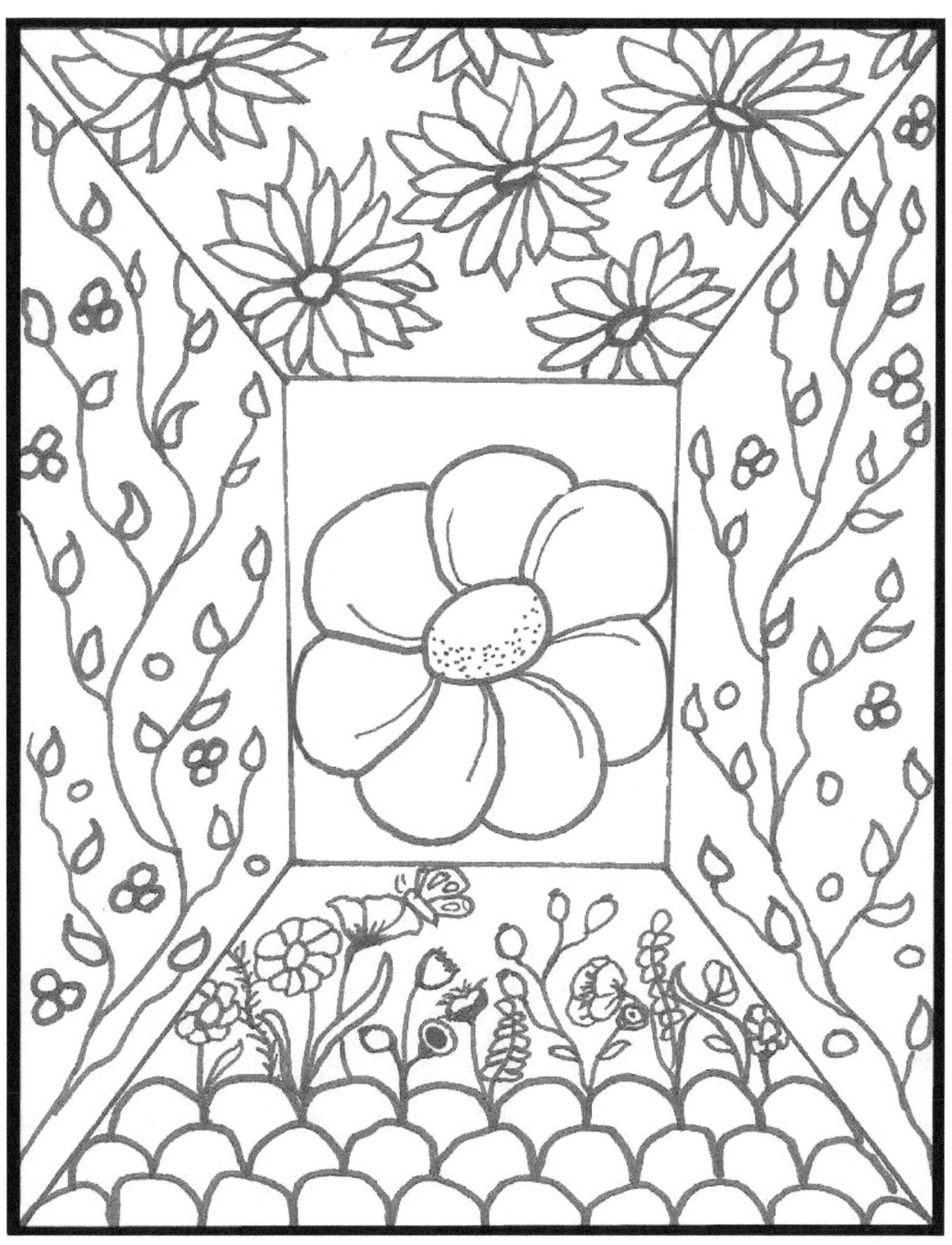

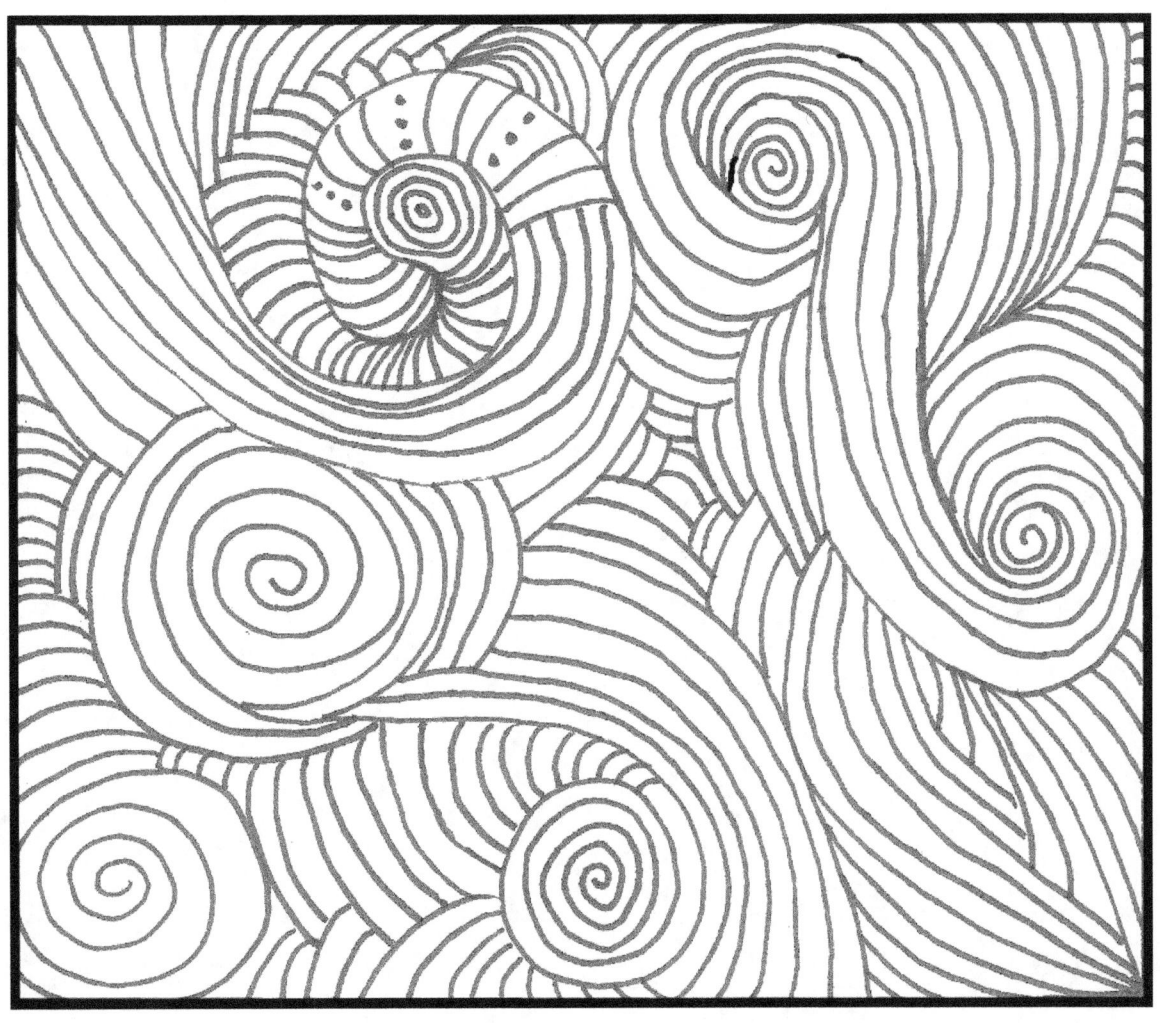

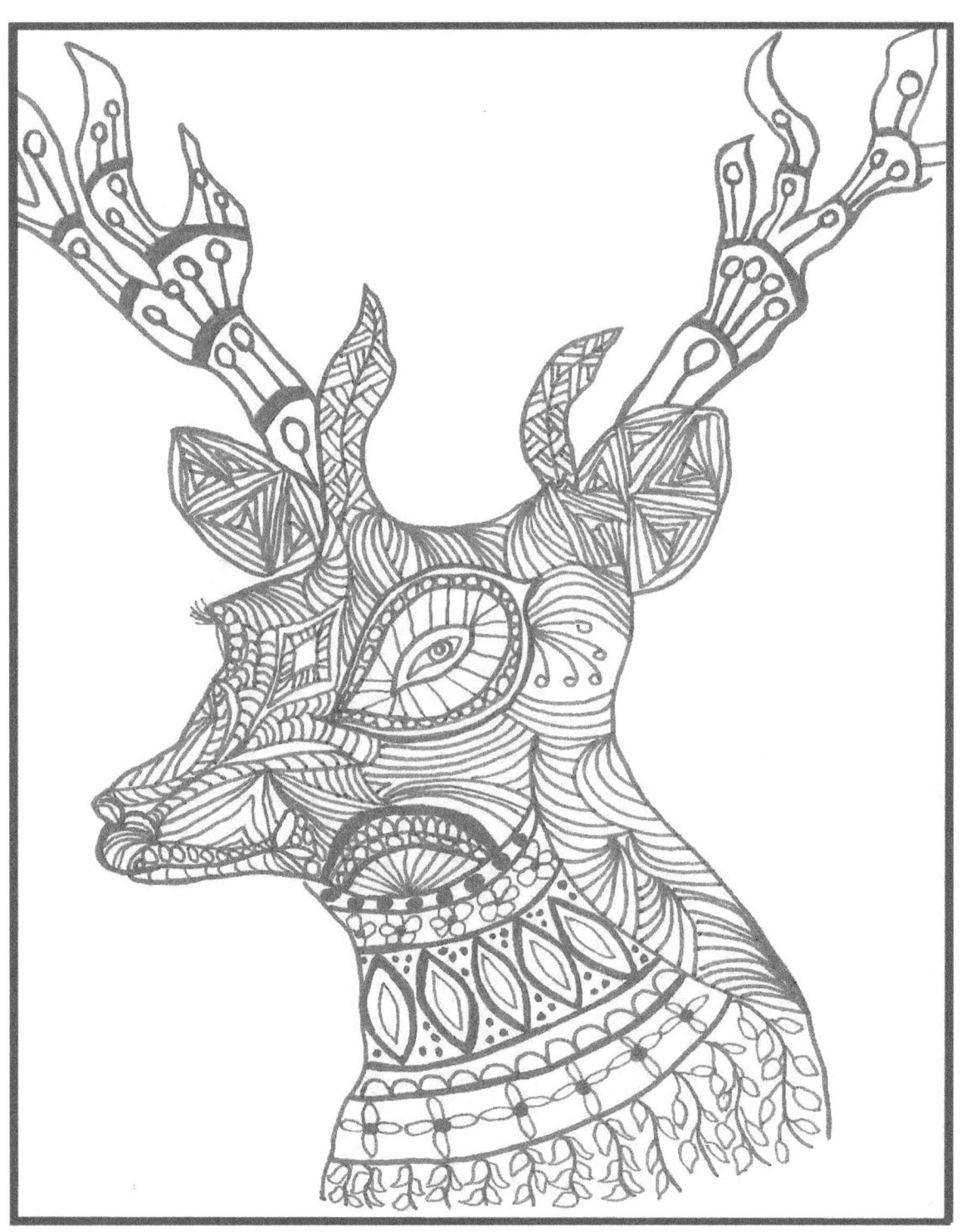

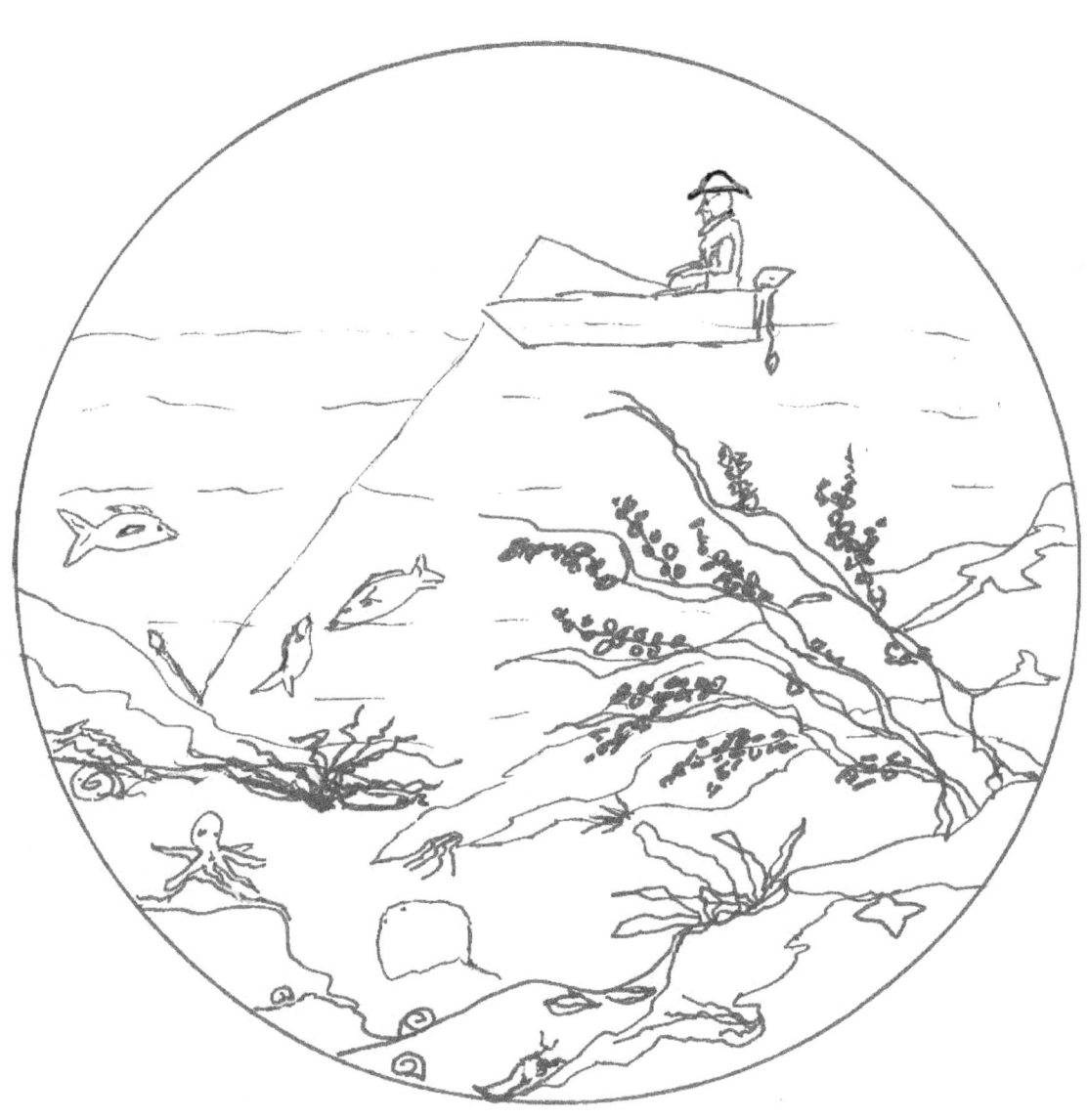

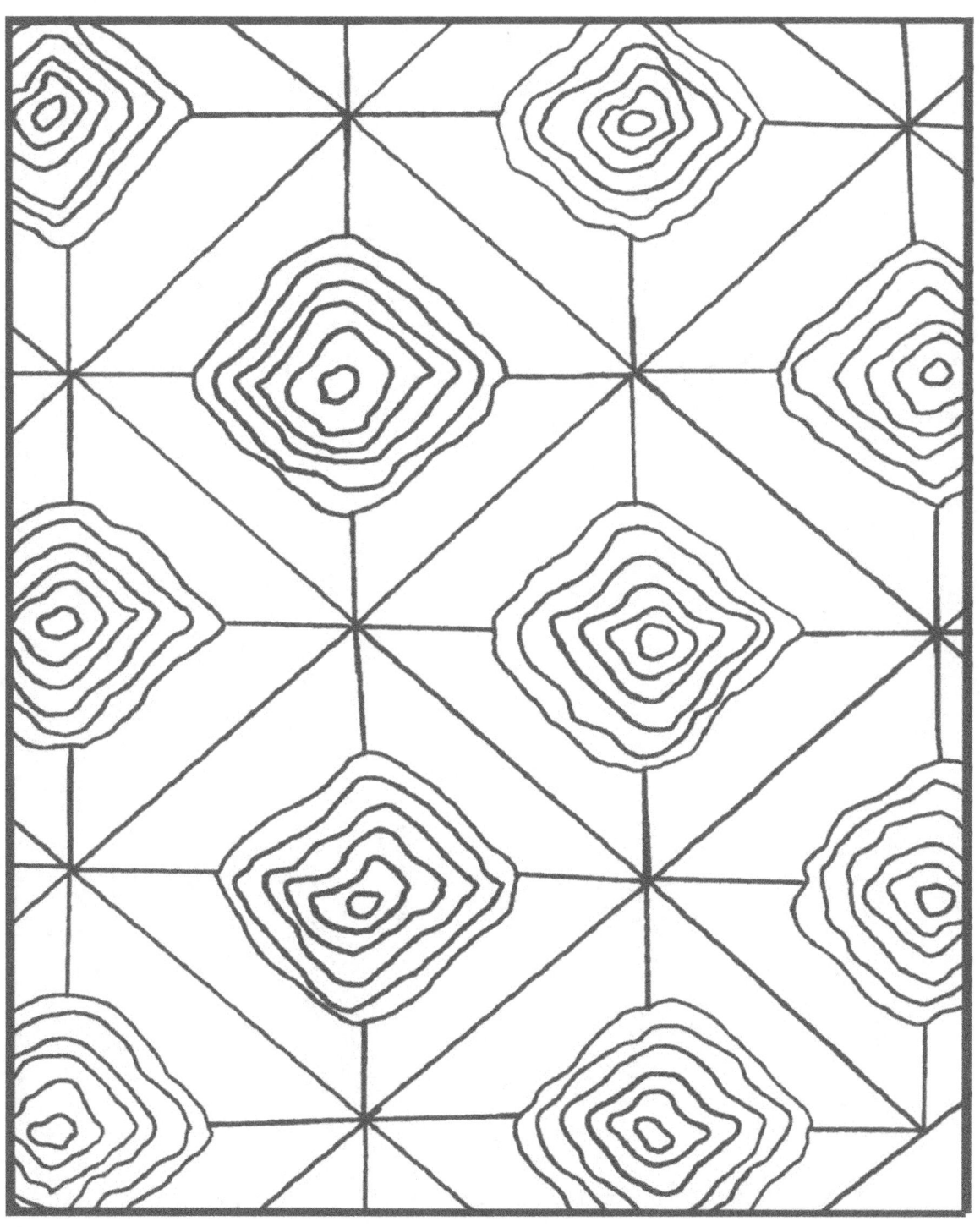

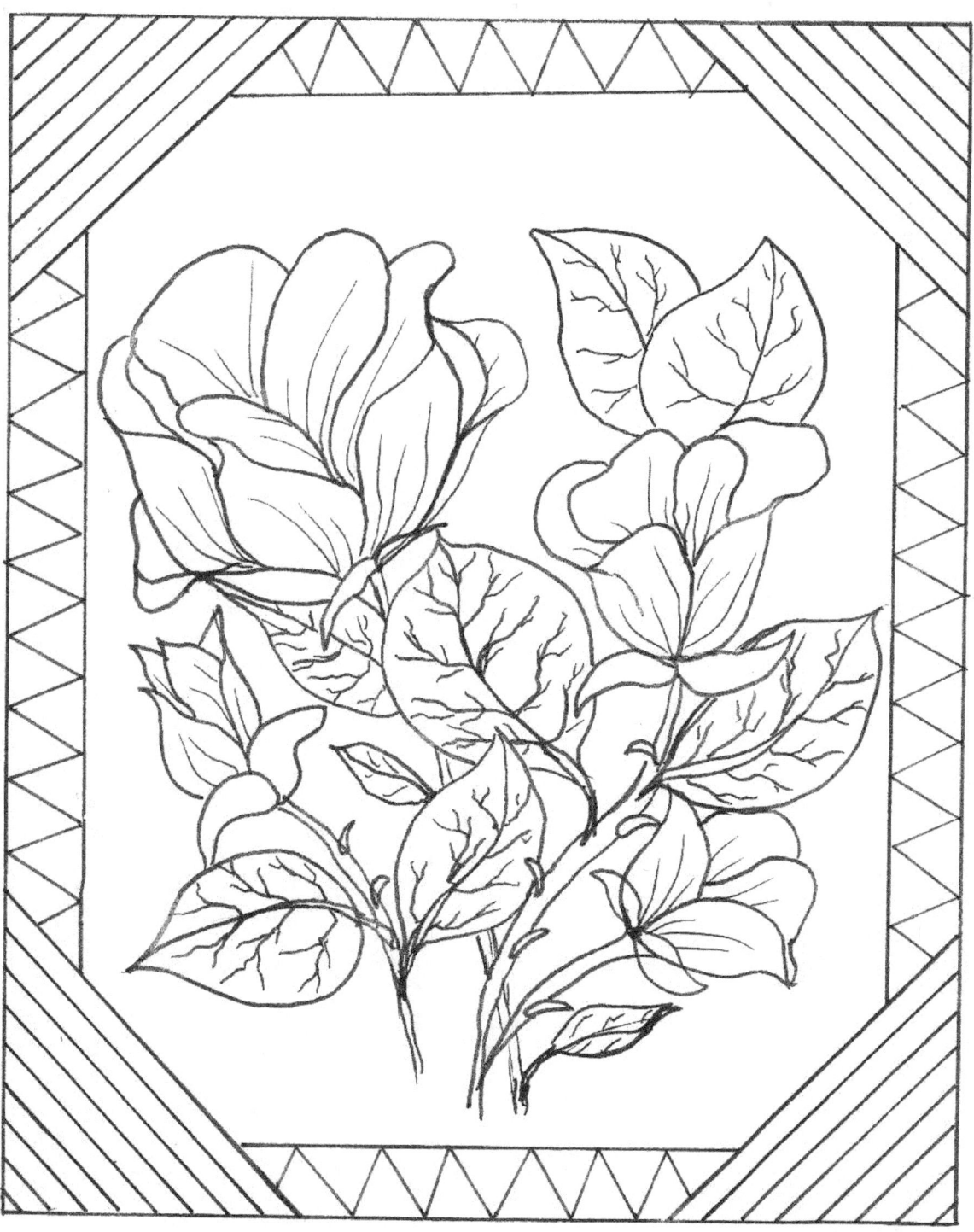

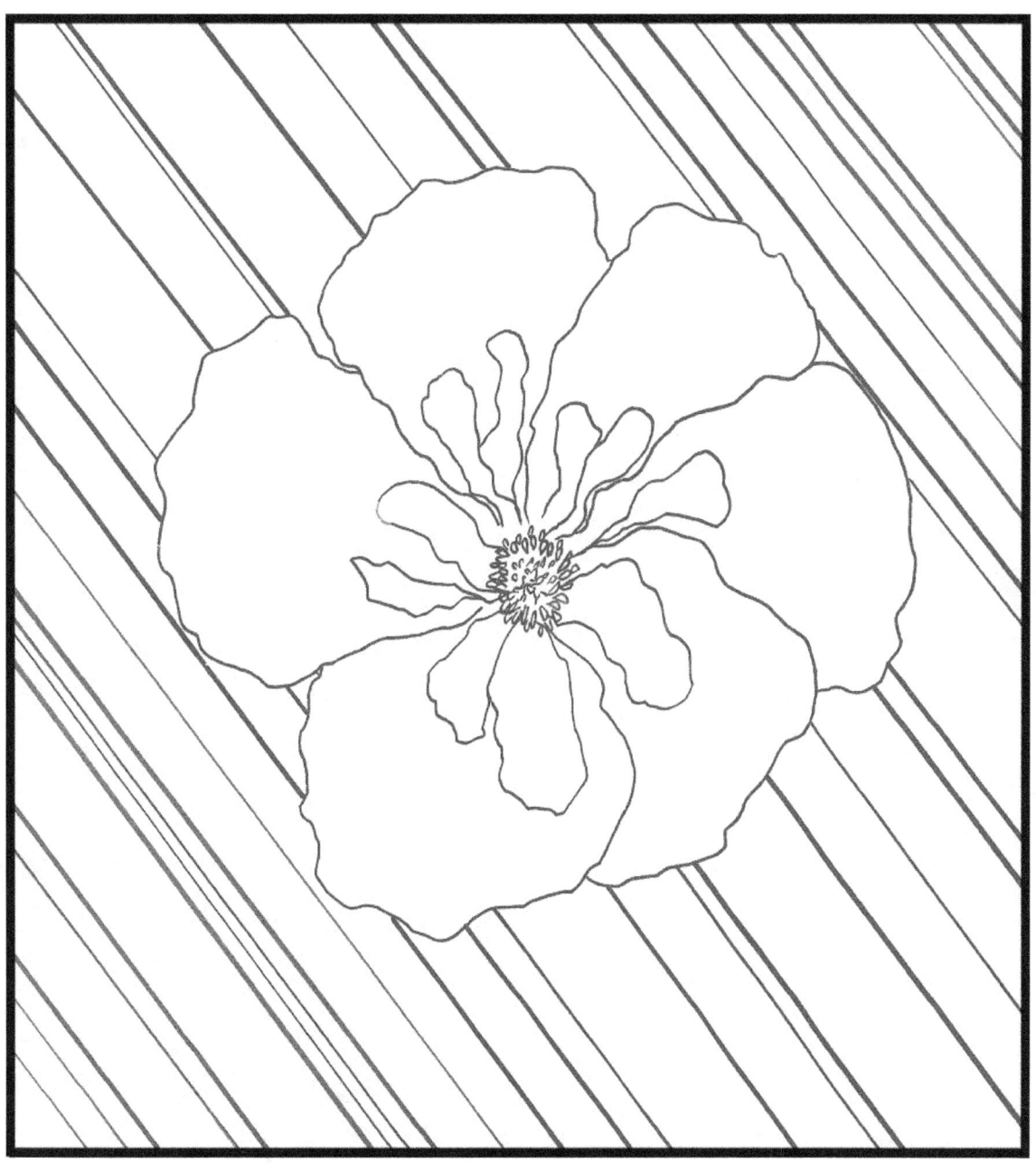

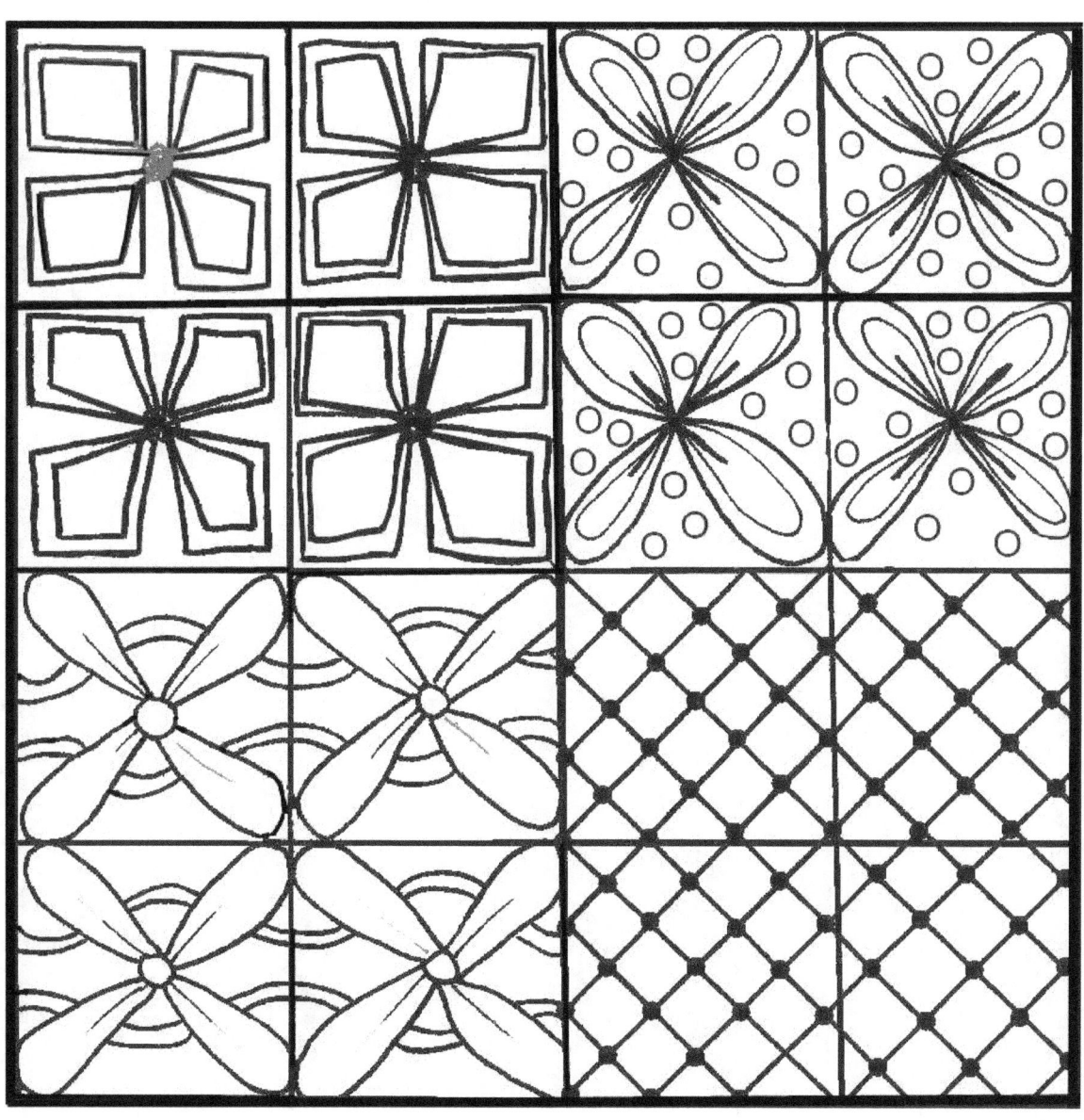

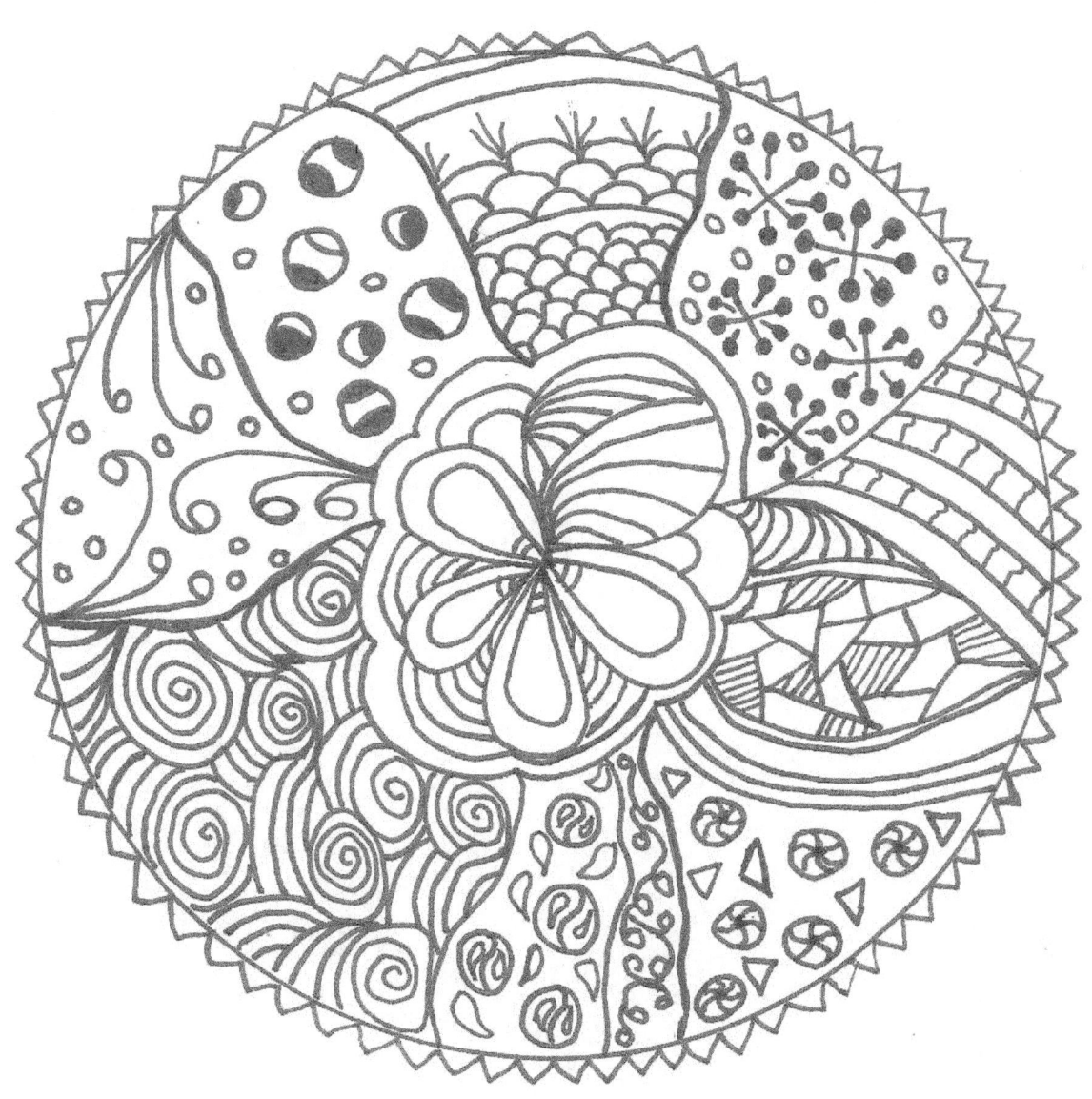

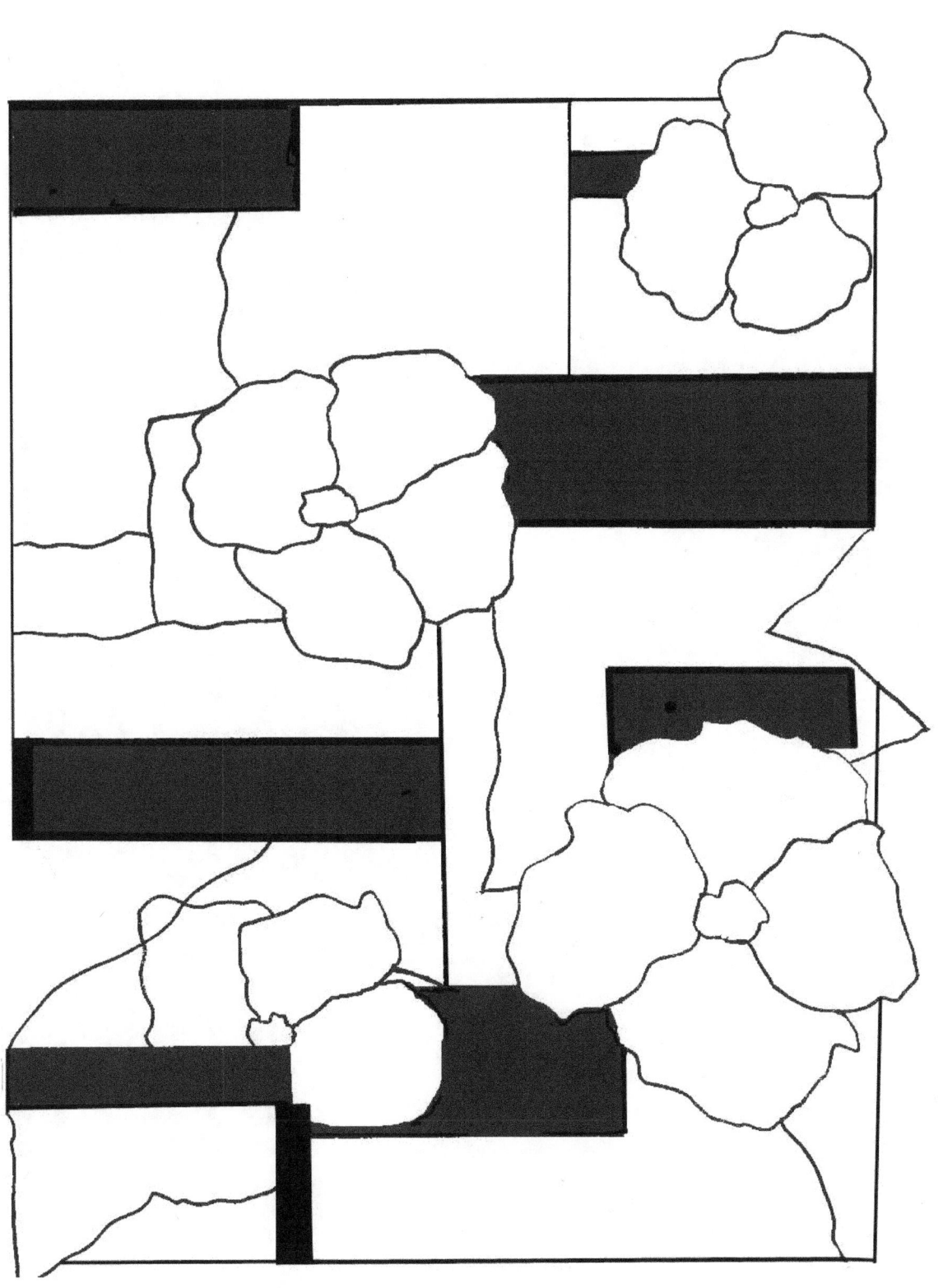

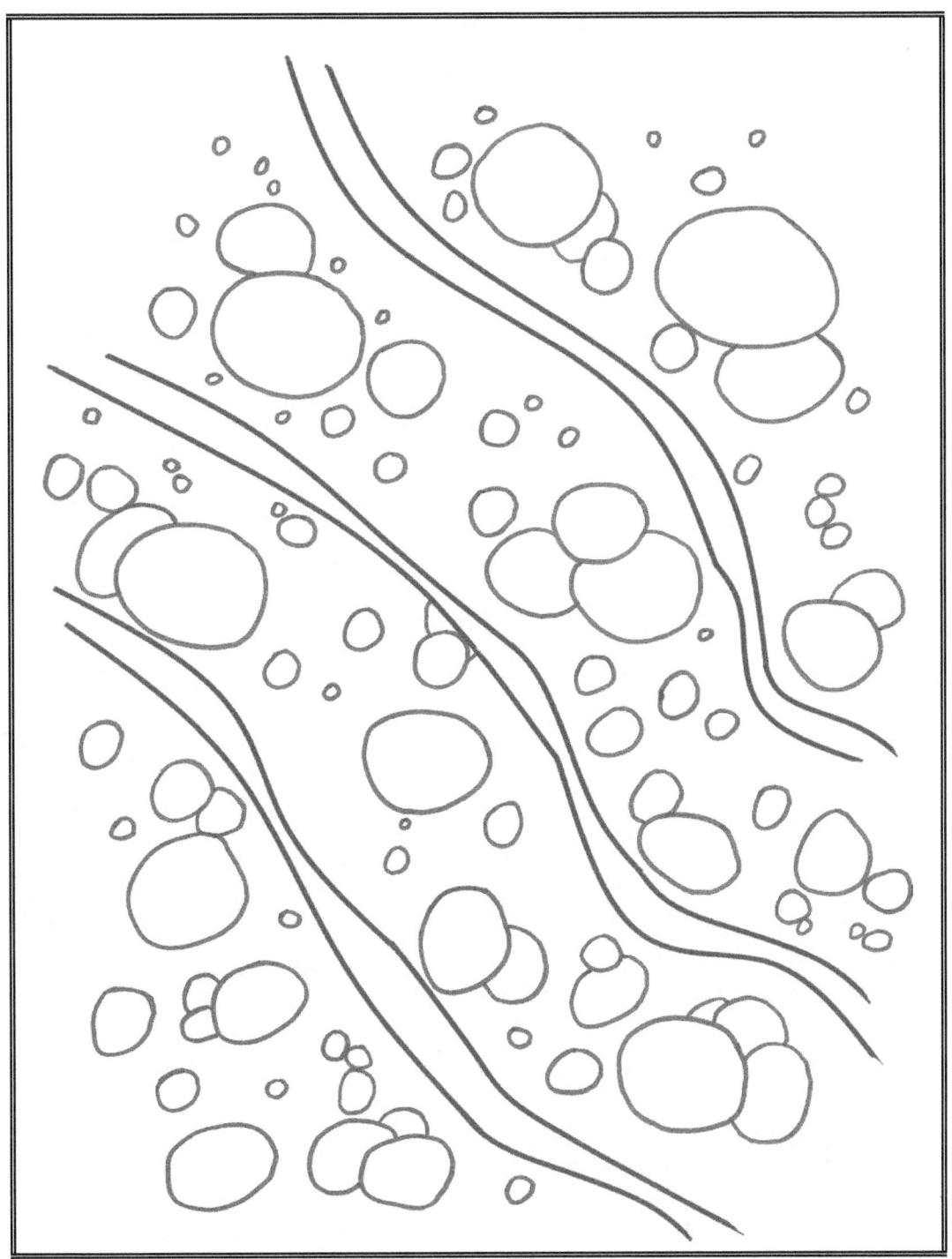

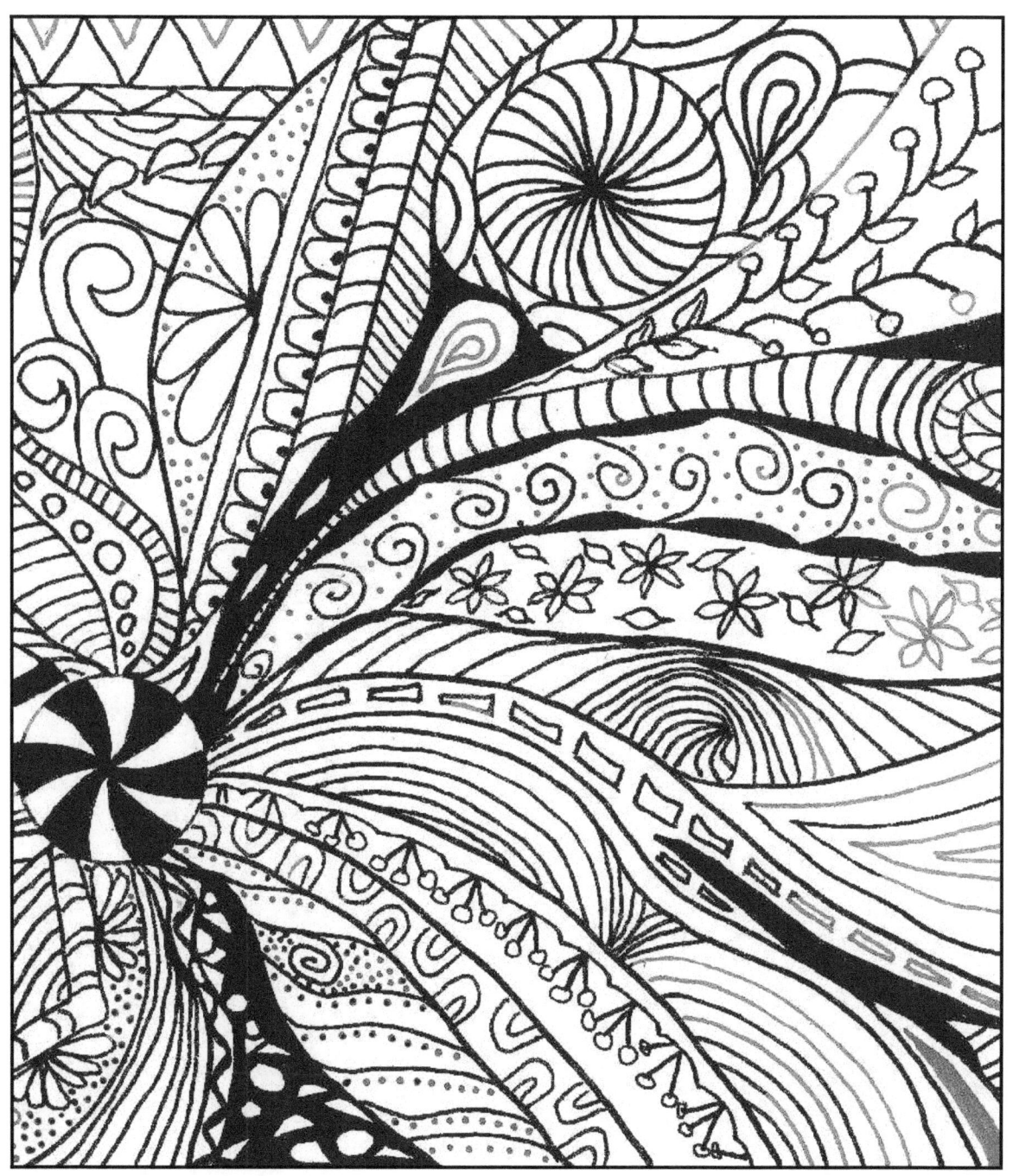

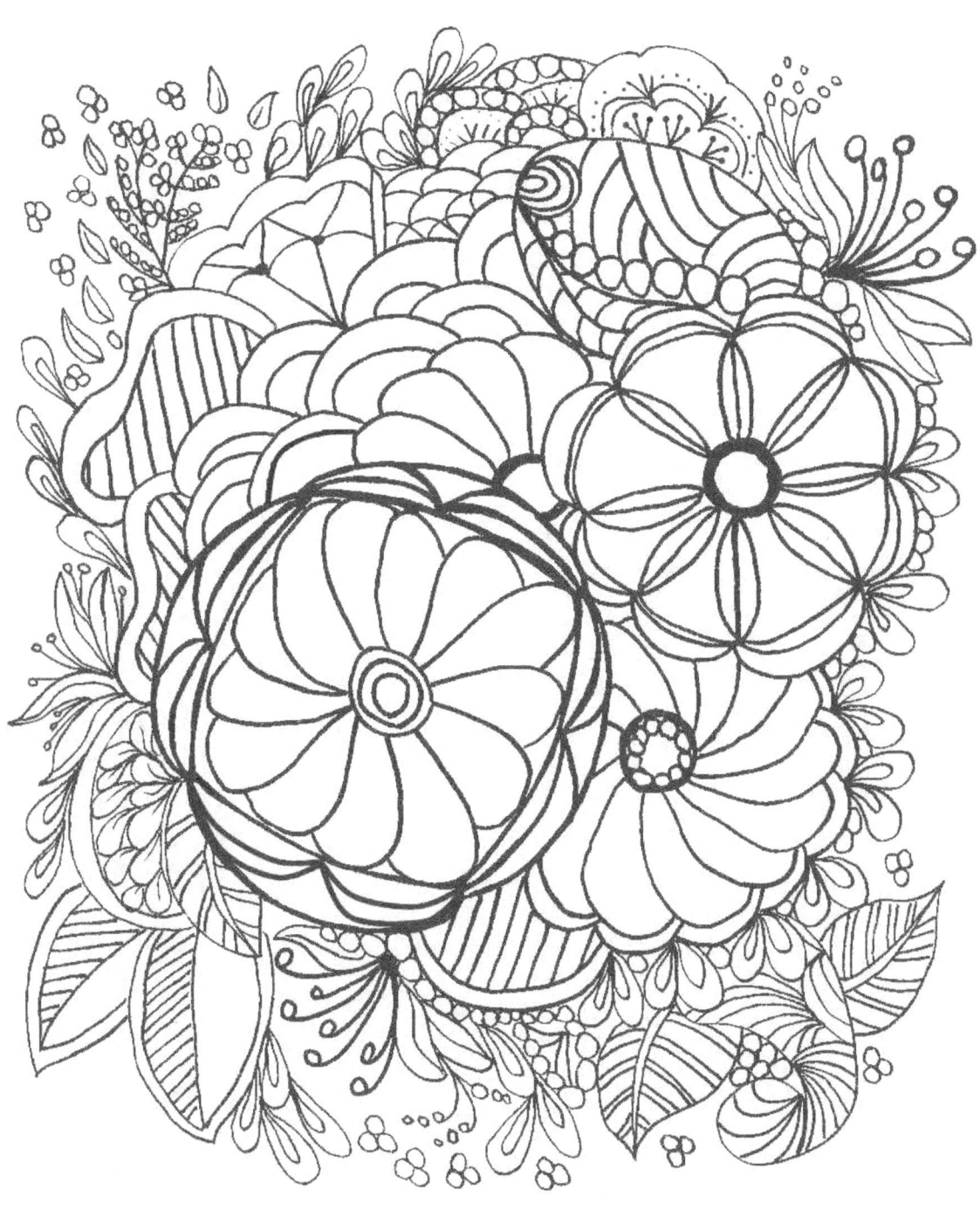

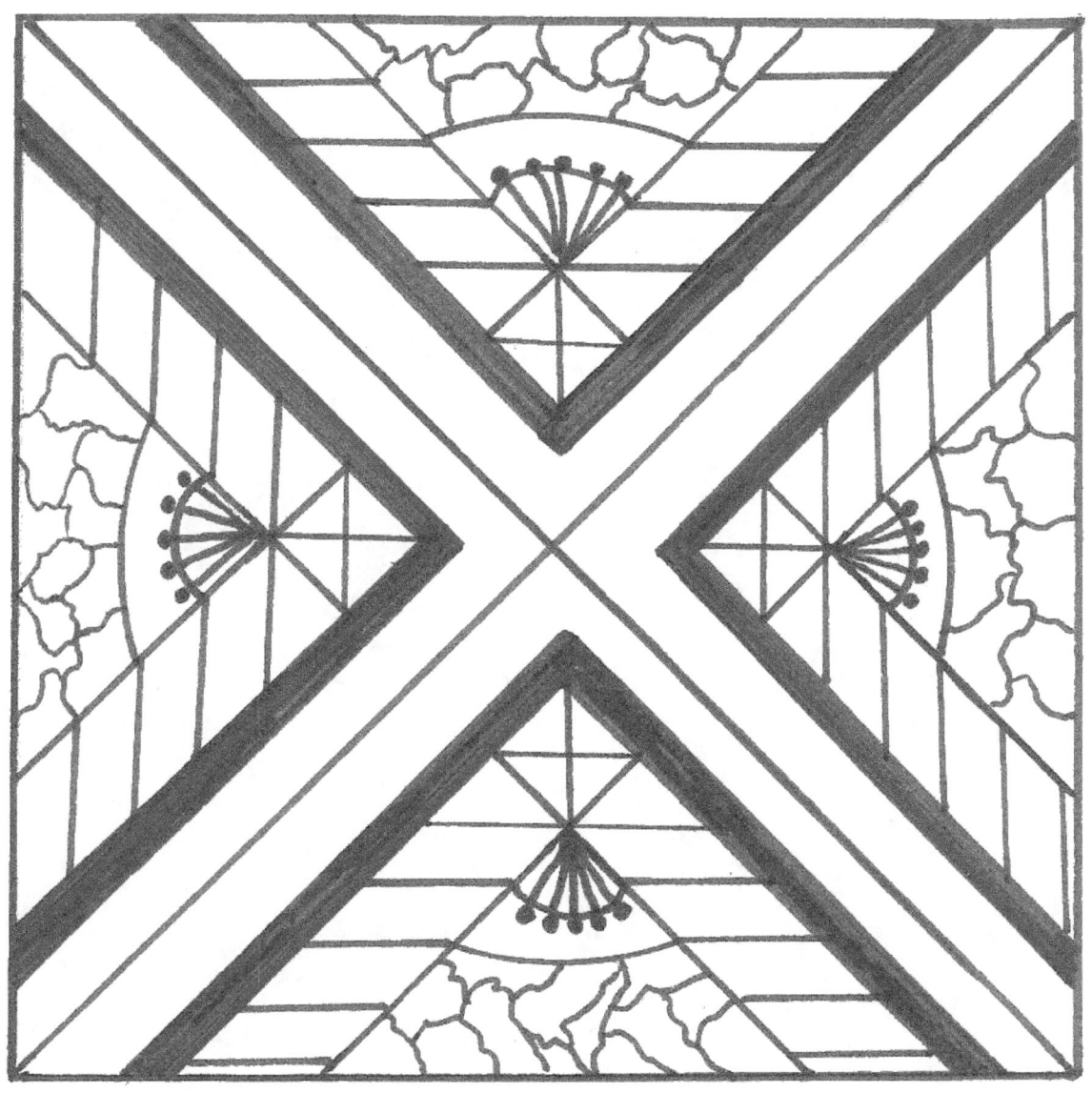

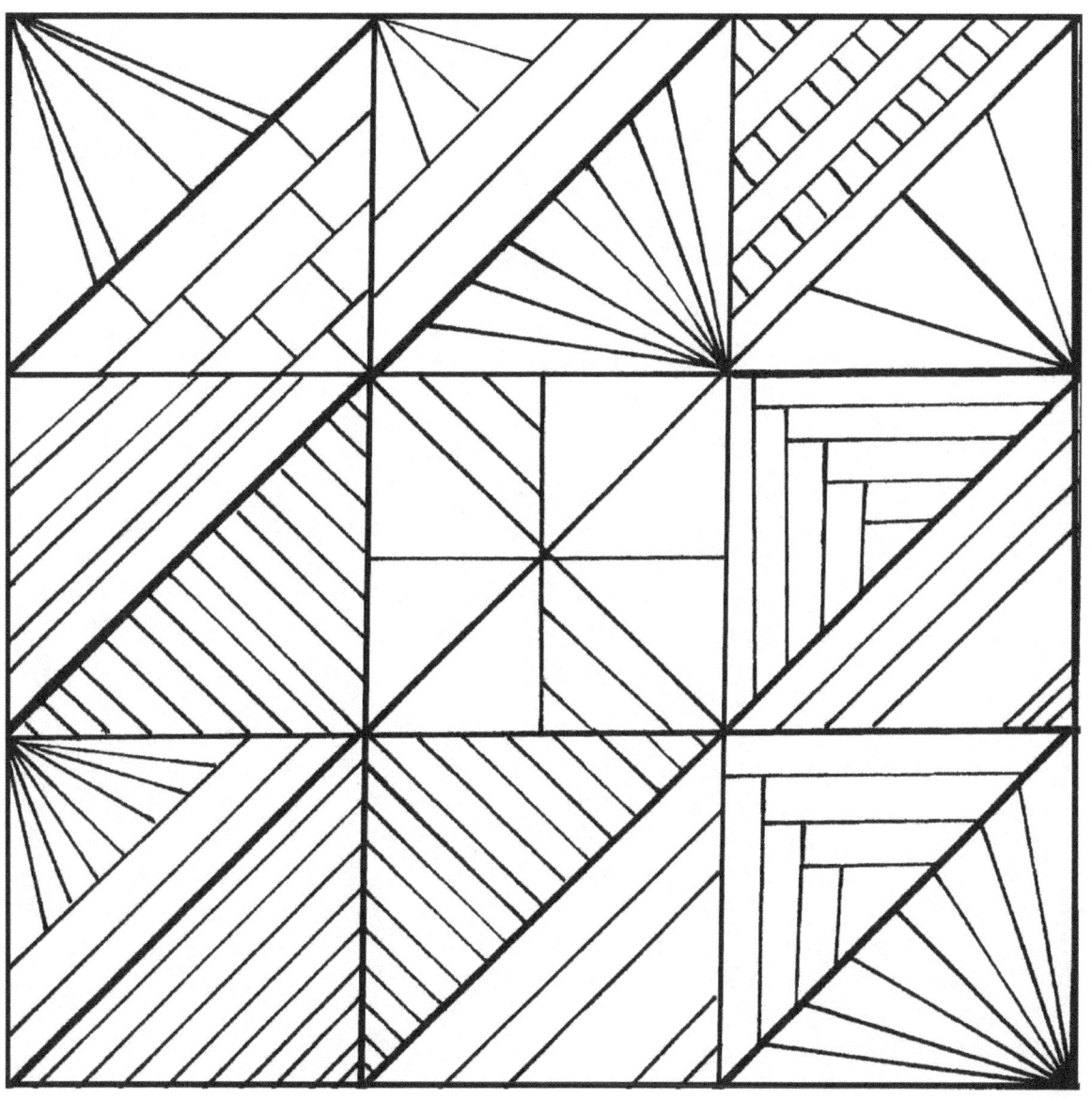

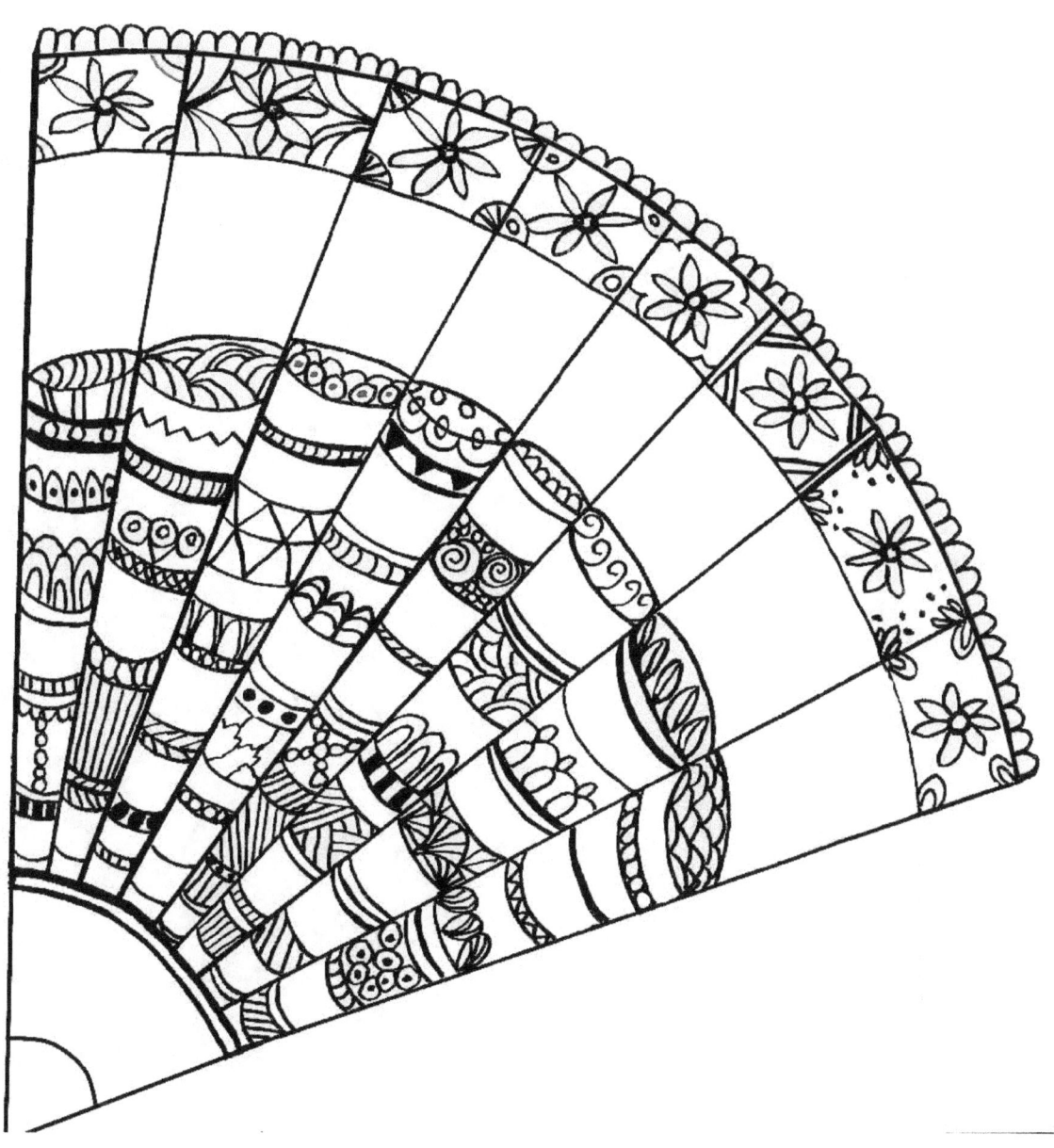

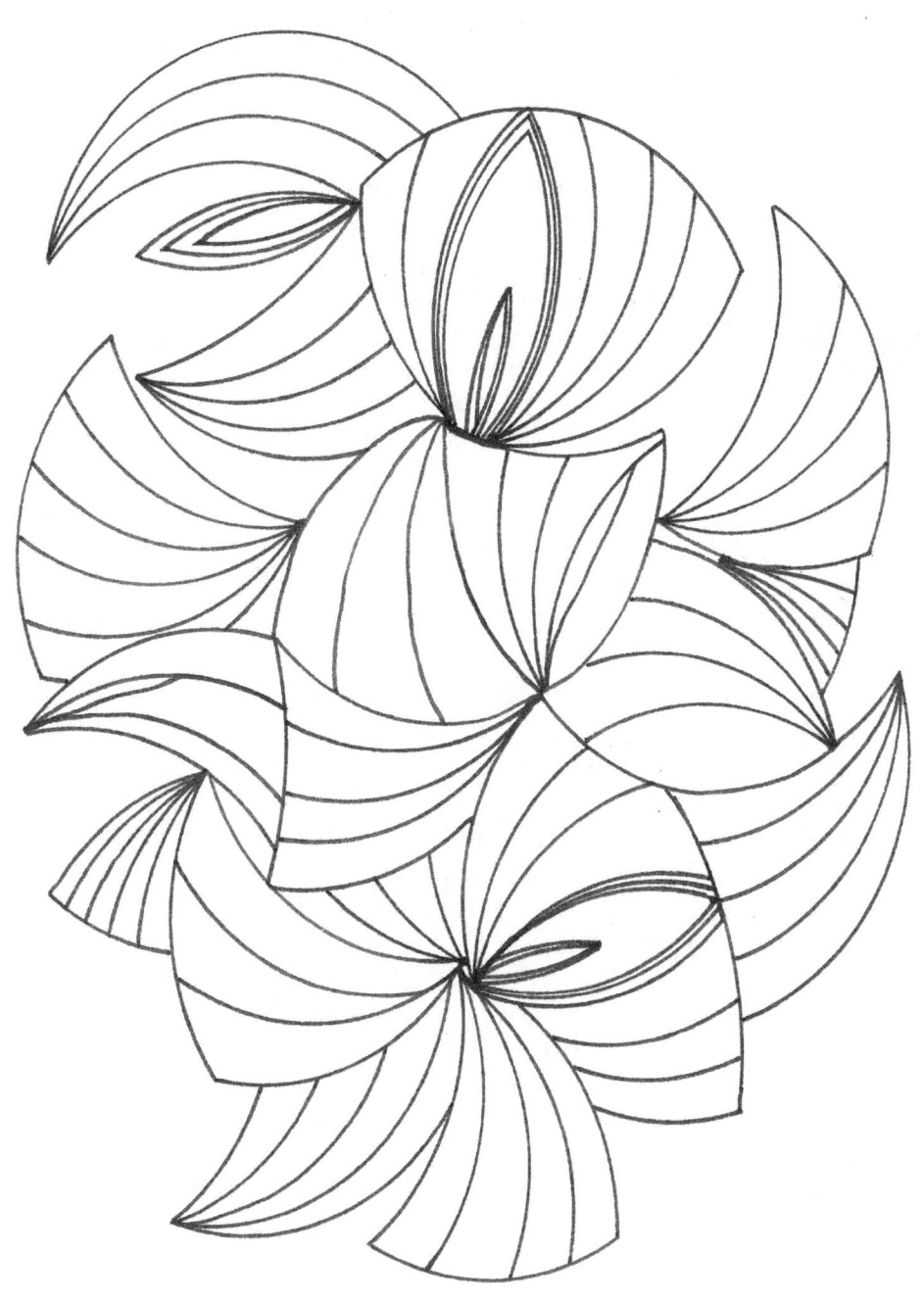

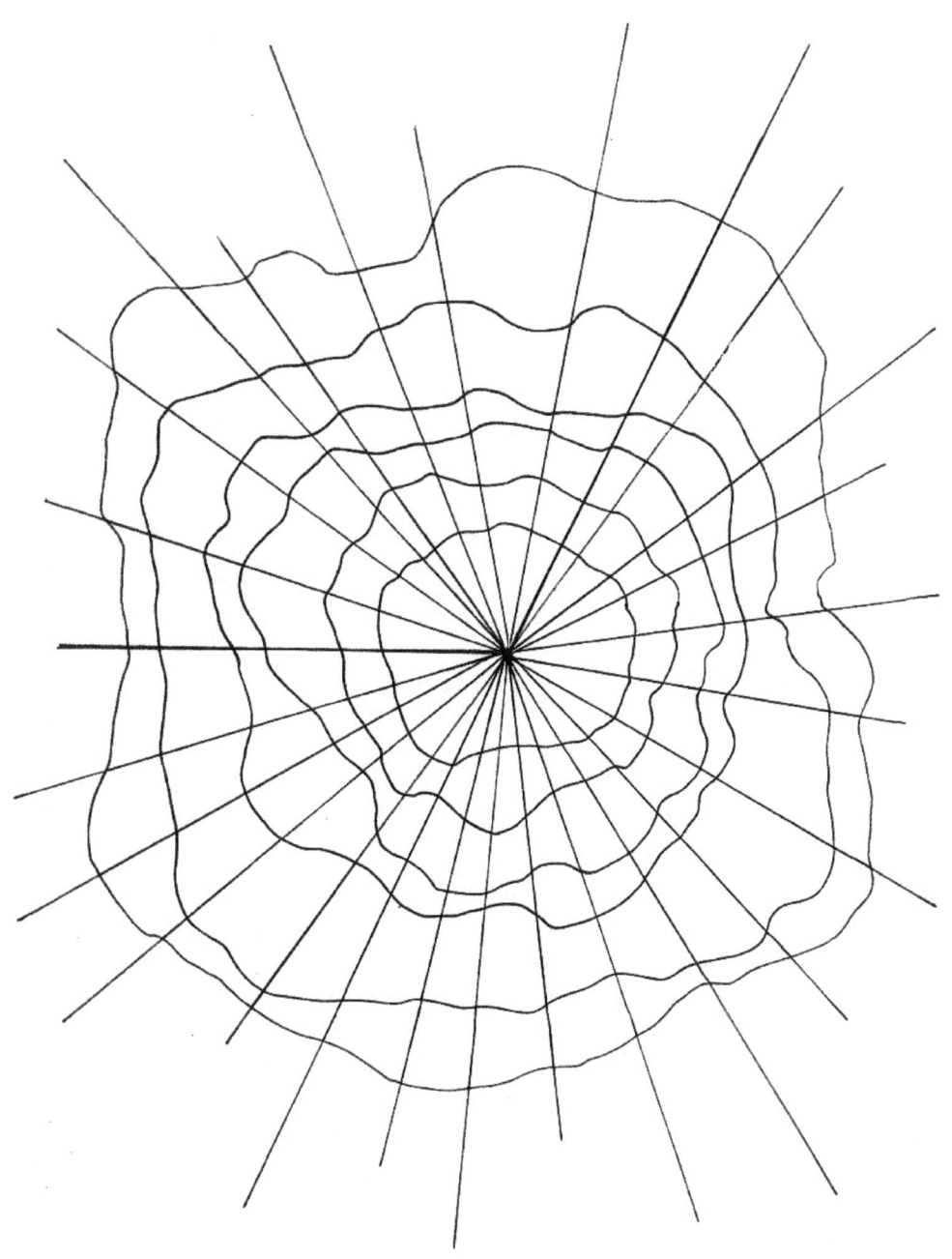

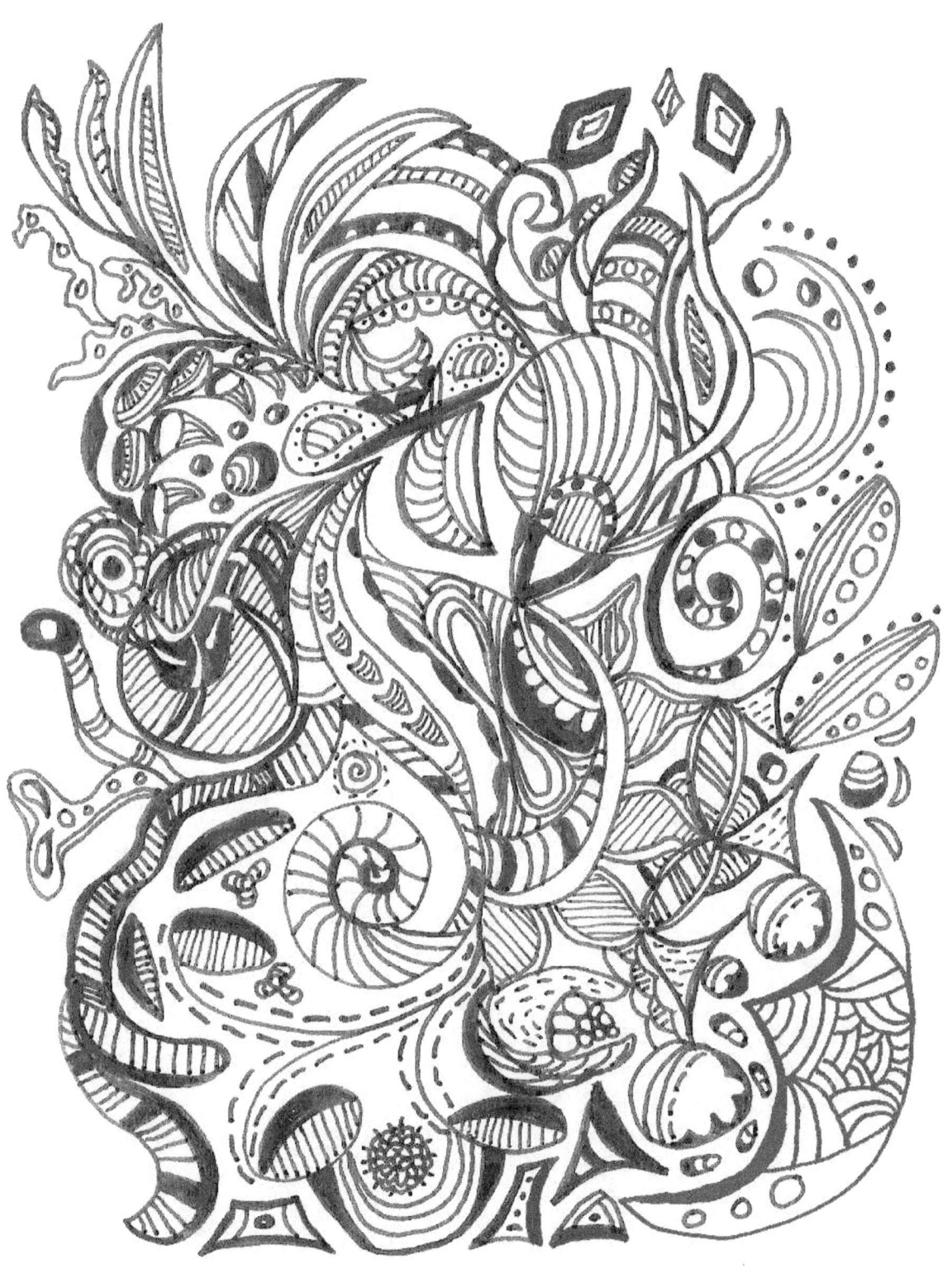

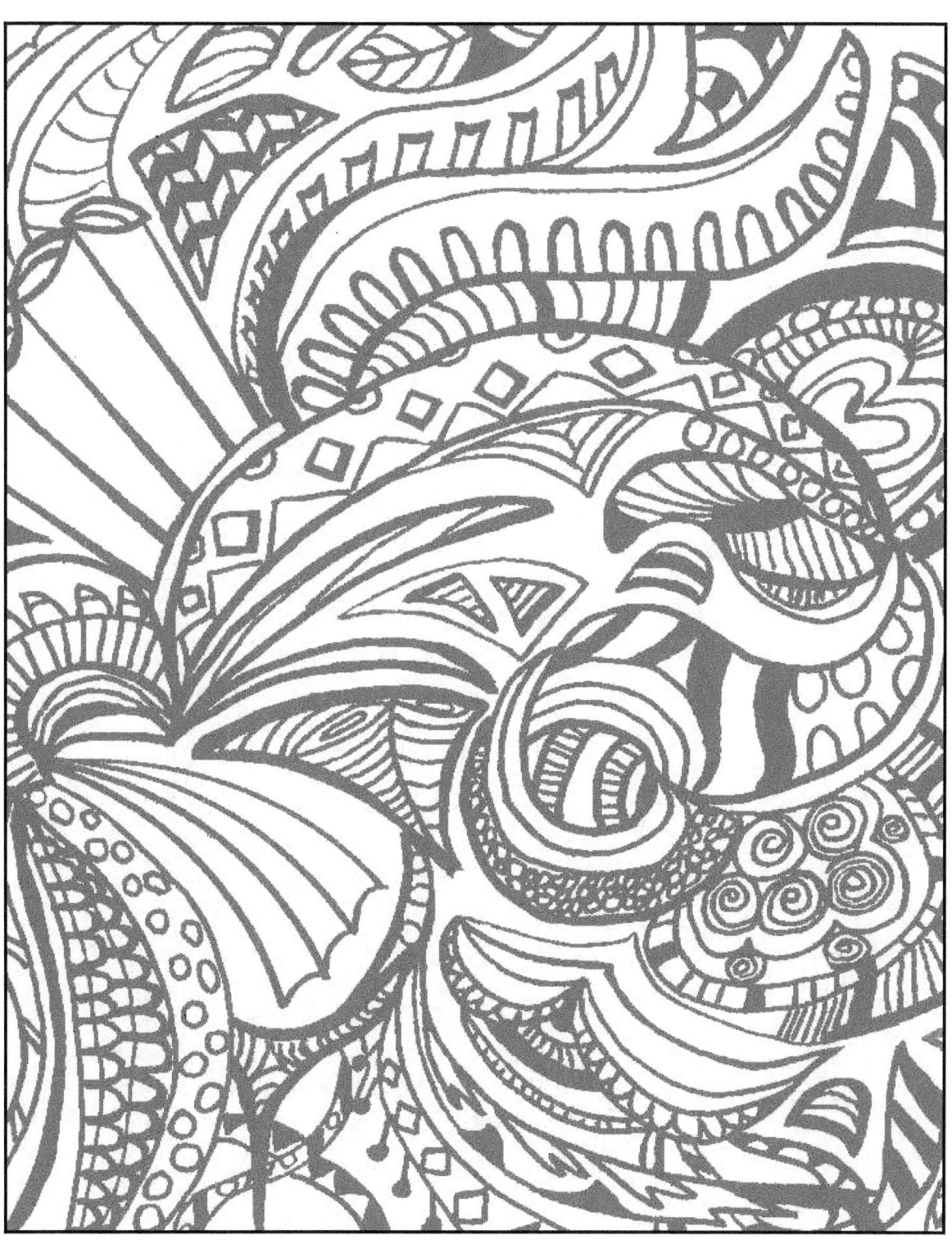

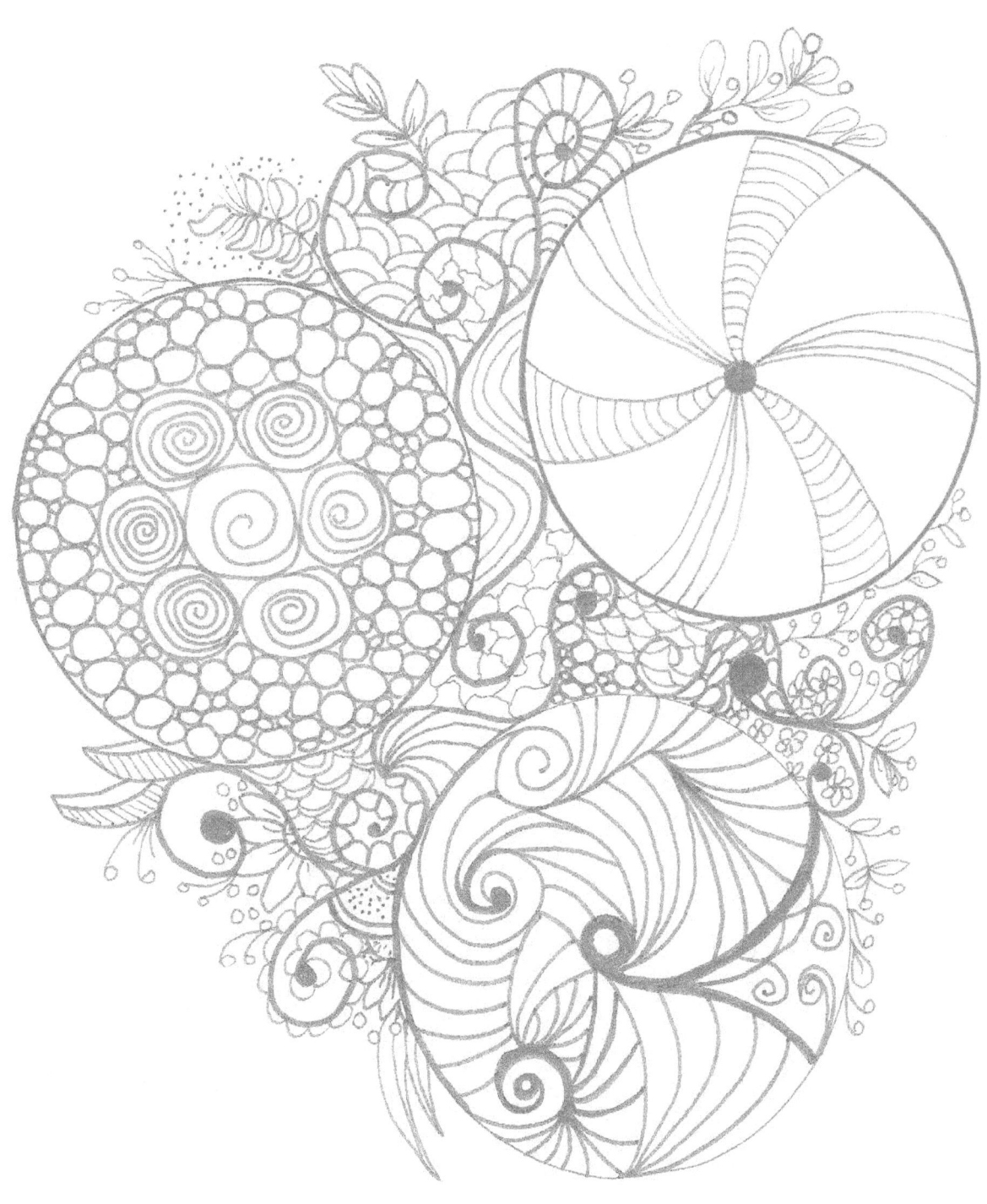

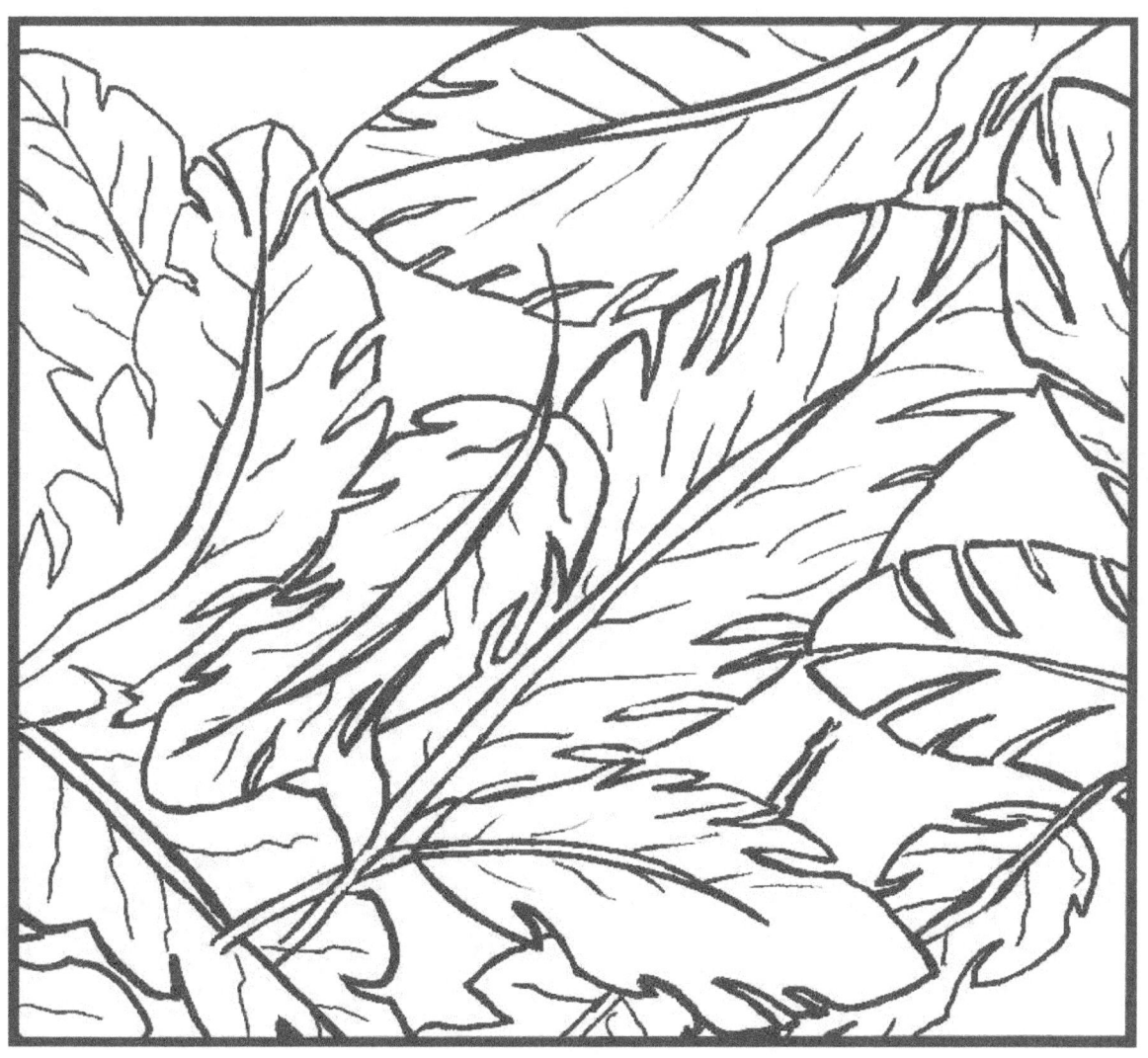

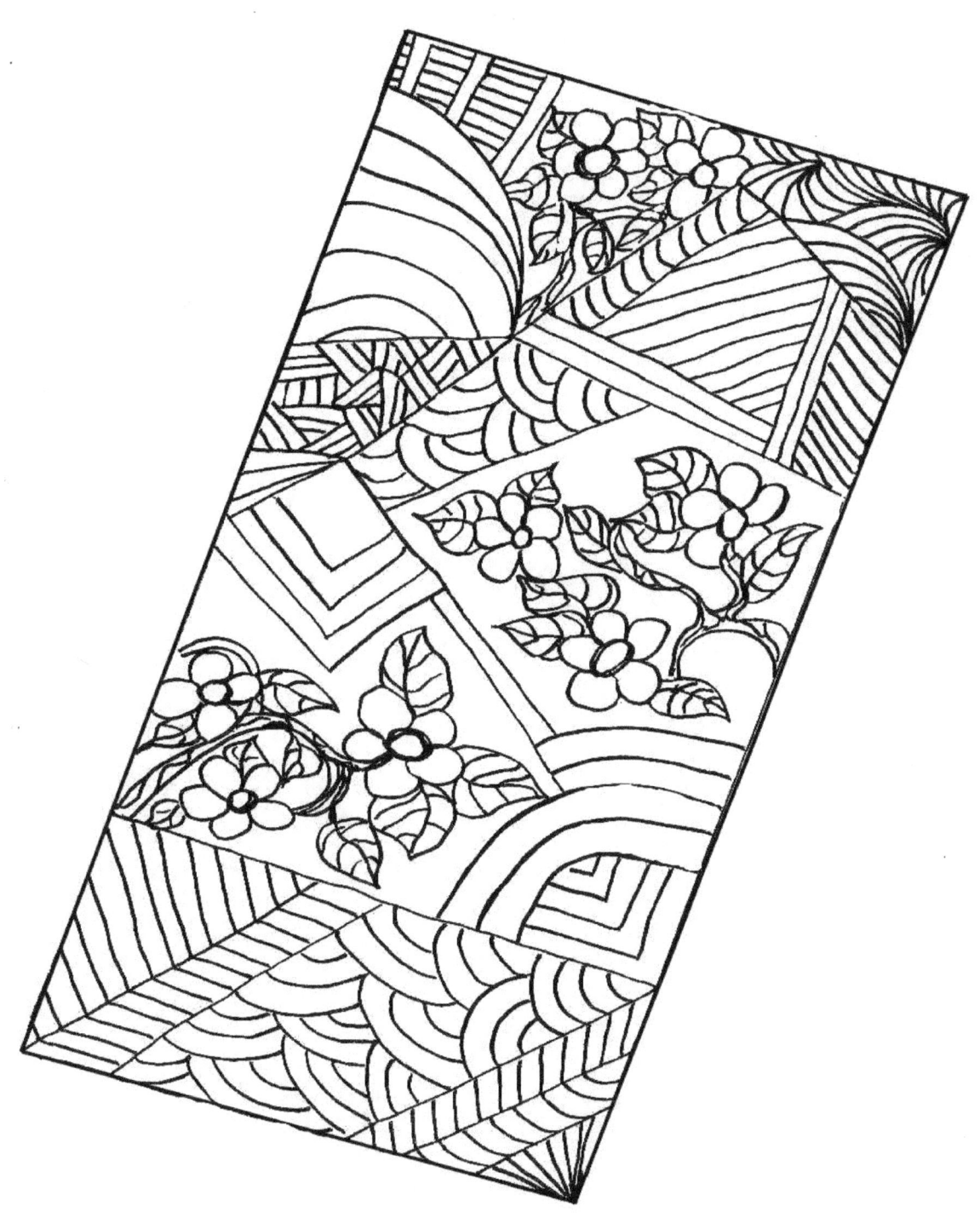

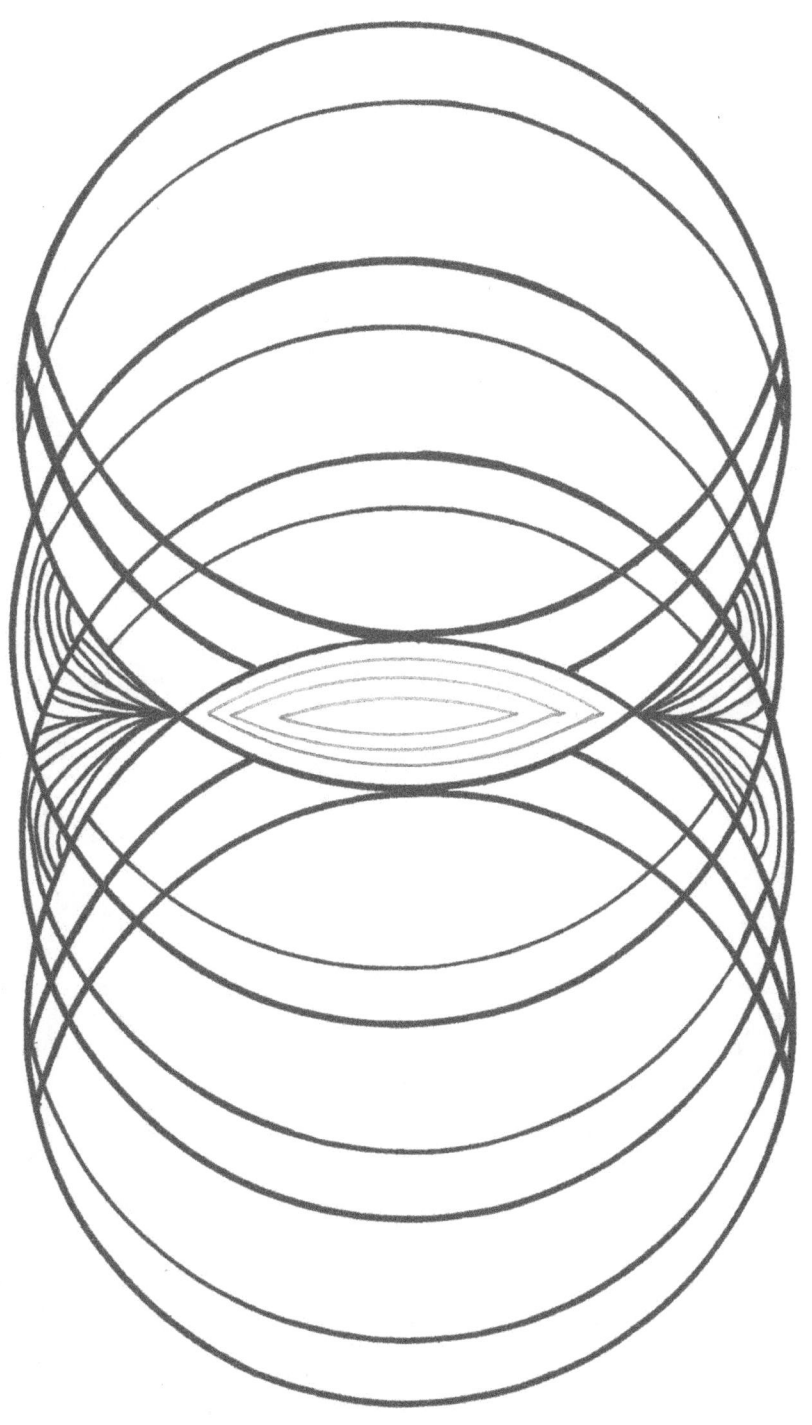

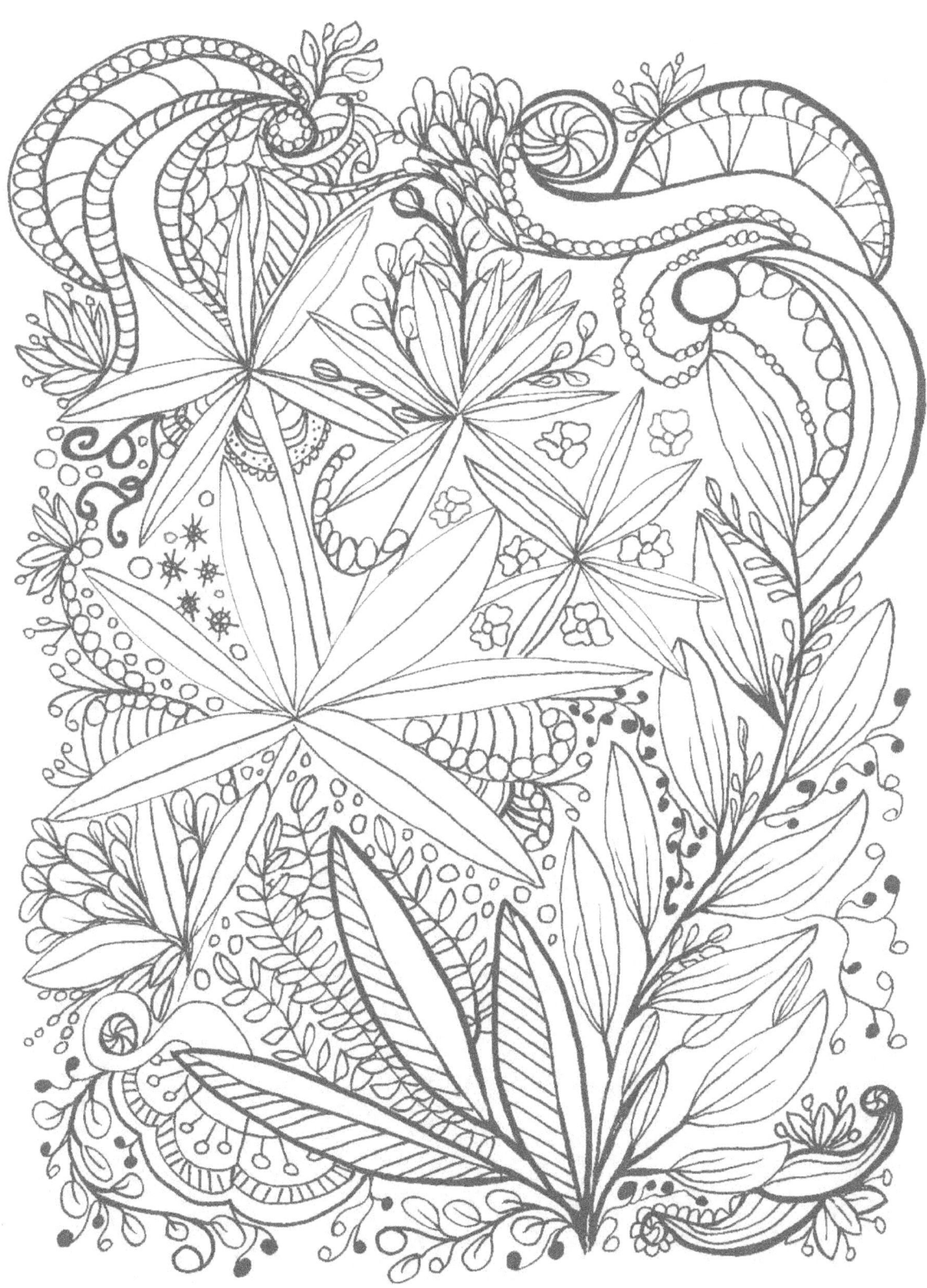

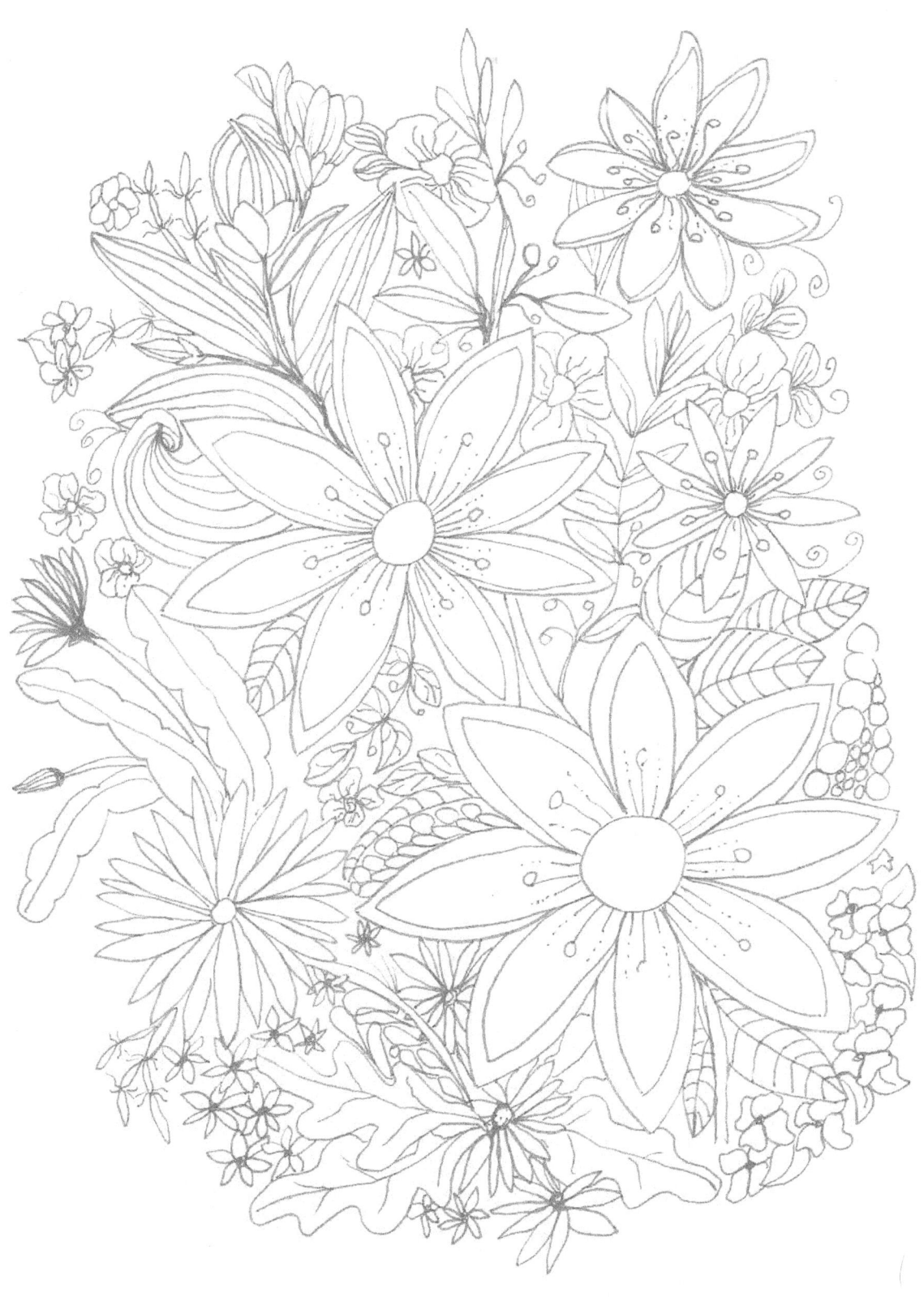

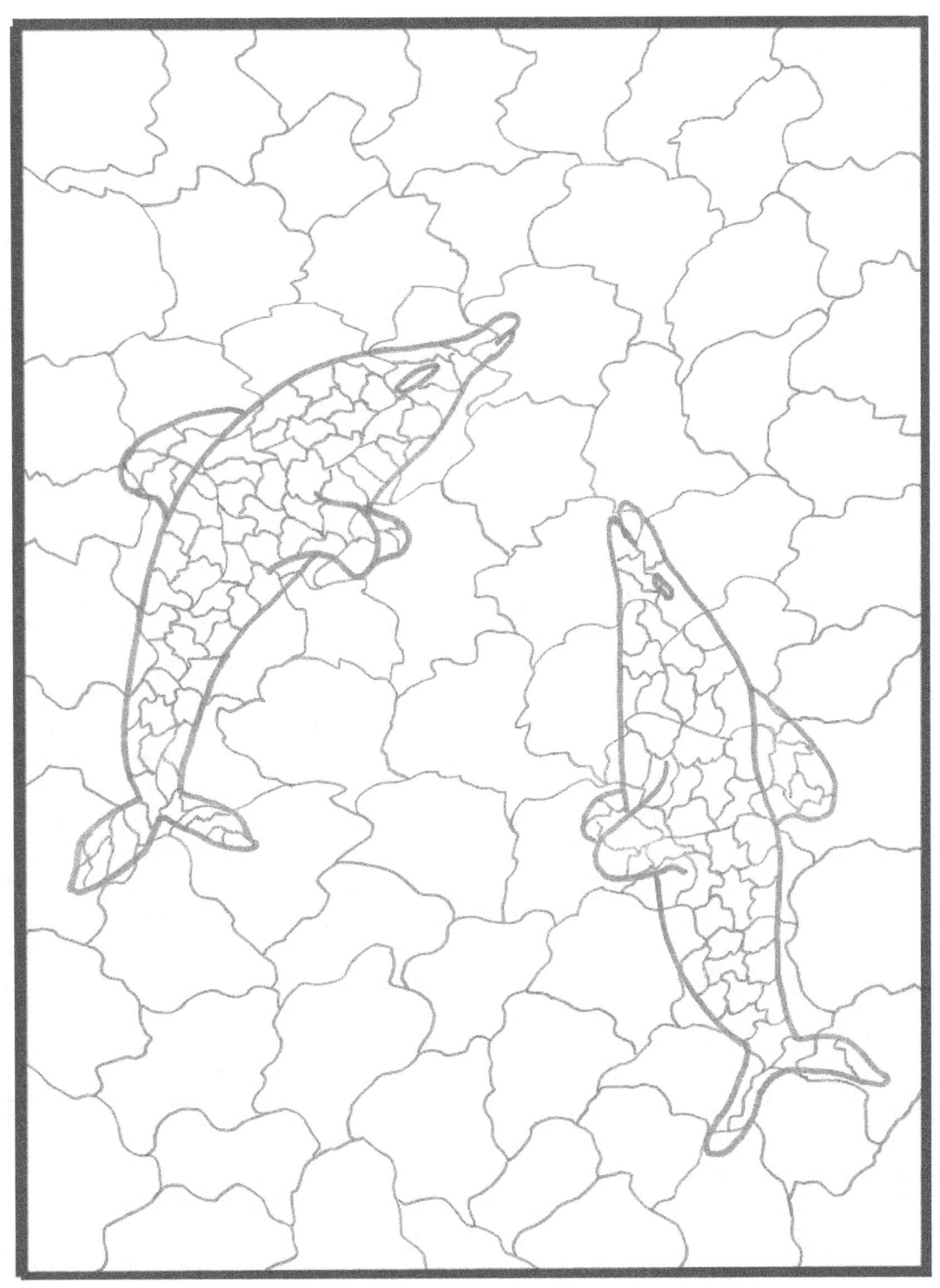

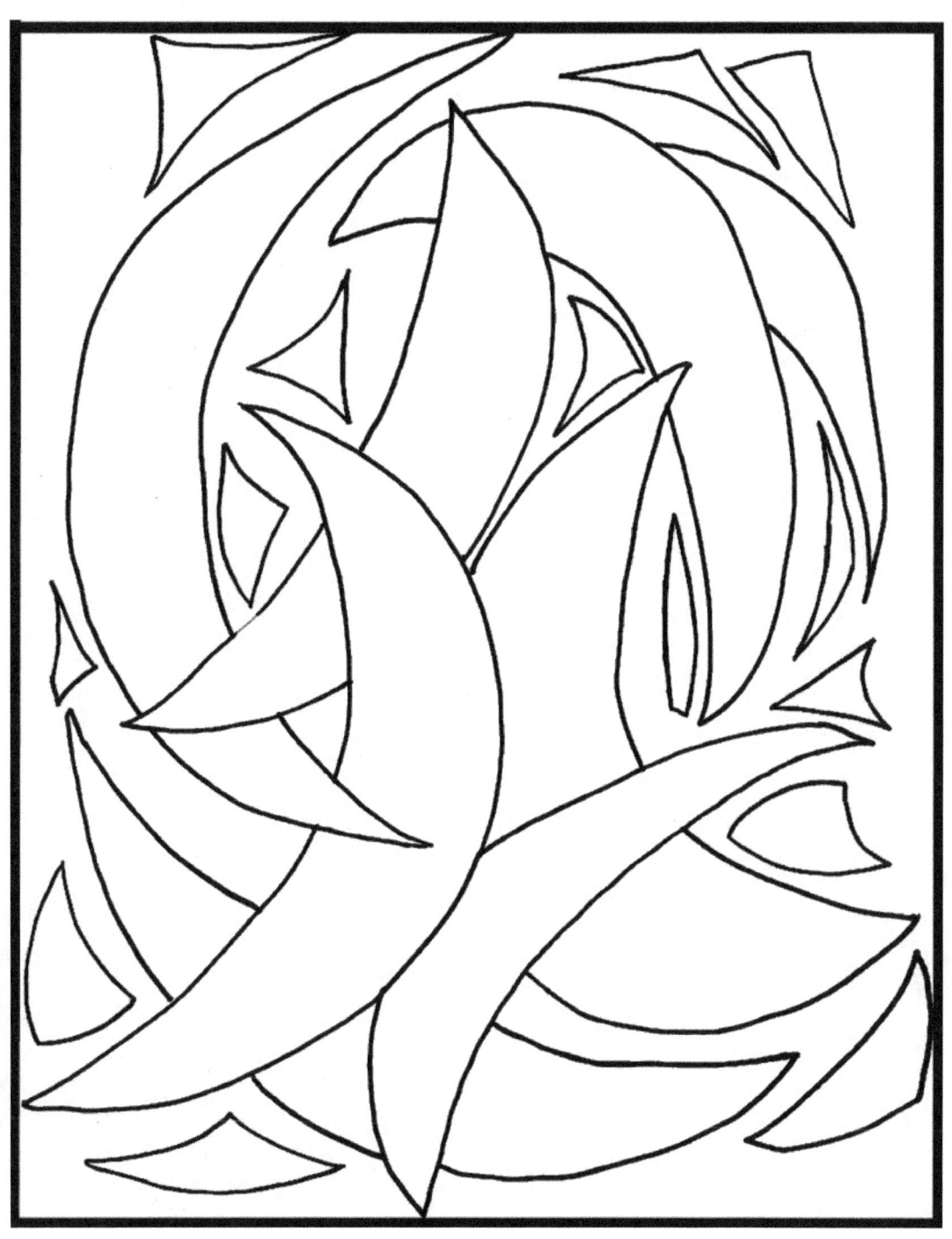

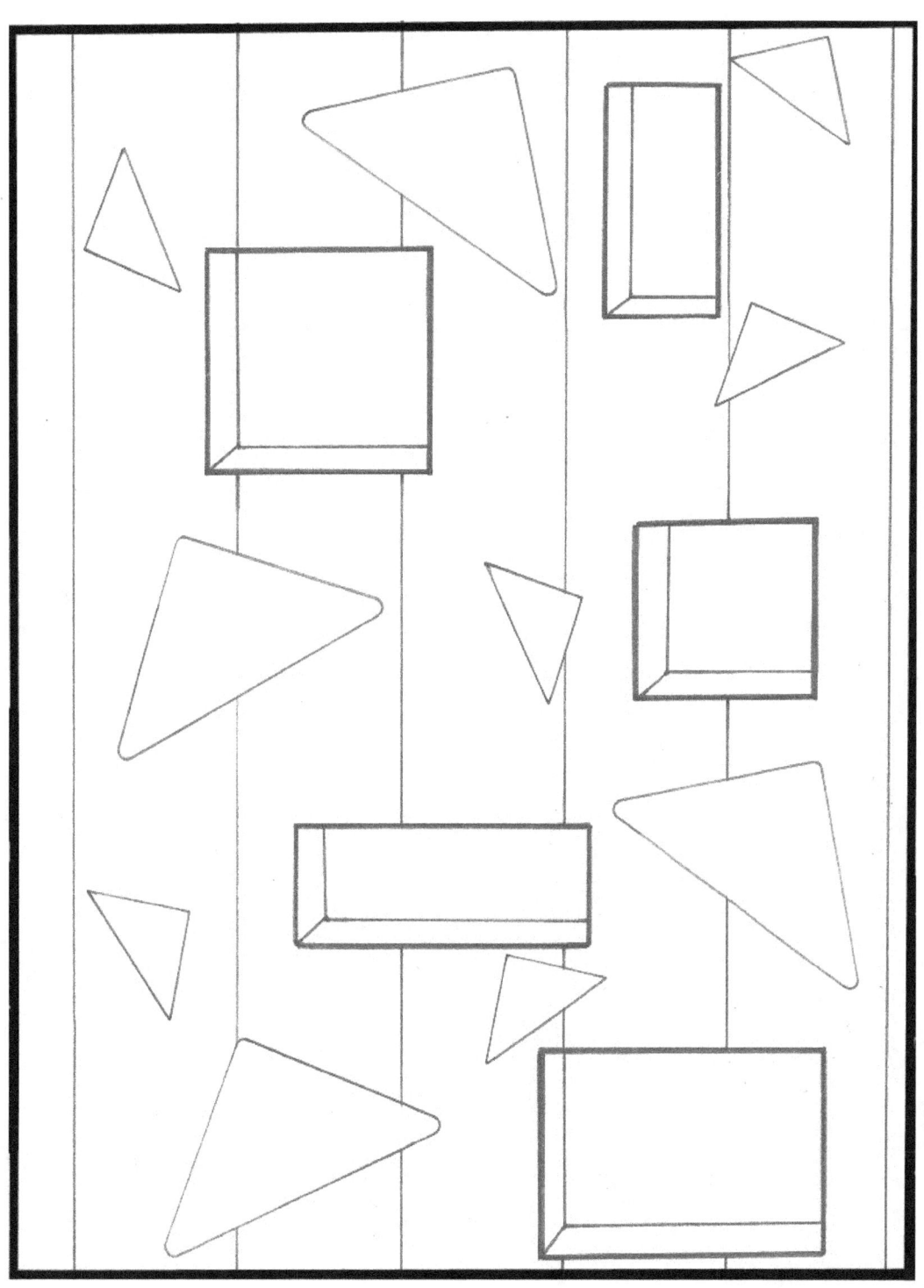

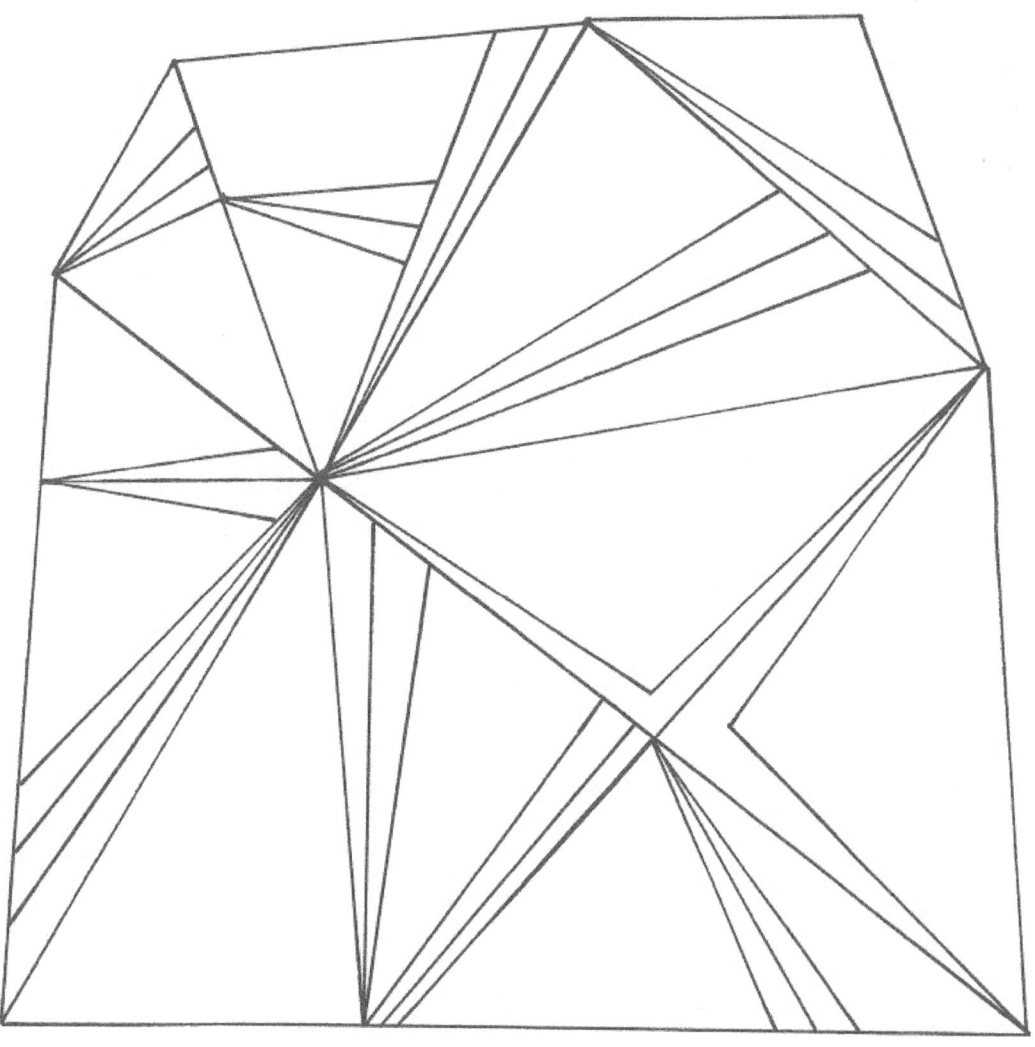

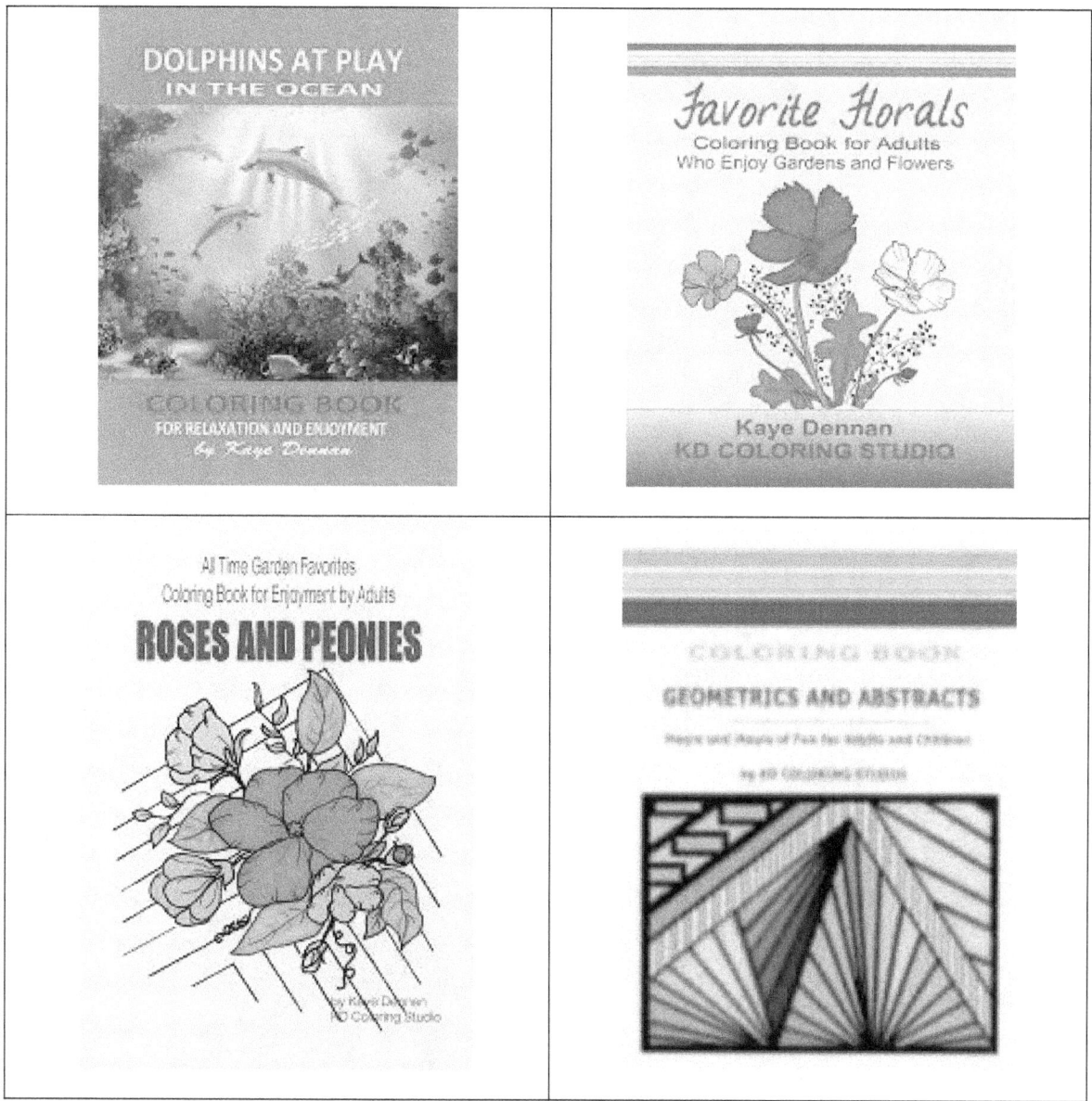

More paperback coloring books can be sourced through

KD COLORING STUDIO AT

http://kdcoloring.com

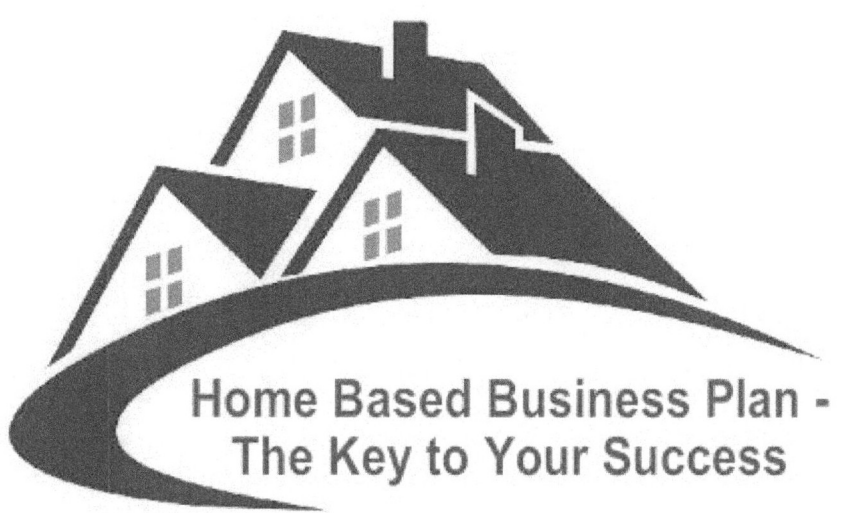

The Home Biz Cafe

Home Based Business Plan -
The Key to Your Success

Home Based Business Courses
by Kaye Dennan
Author and Home Business Expert
http://thehomebizcafe.com